Paul
as Pastor

Text copyright © Patrick Whitworth 2012
The author asserts the moral right
to be identified as the author of this work

Published by
The Bible Reading Fellowship
15 The Chambers, Vineyard
Abingdon OX14 3FE
United Kingdom
Tel: +44 (0)1865 319700
Email: enquiries@brf.org.uk
Website: www.brf.org.uk
BRF is a Registered Charity

ISBN 978 0 85746 046 2
First published 2012
10 9 8 7 6 5 4 3 2 1 0
All rights reserved

Acknowledgments
Unless otherwise stated, scripture quotations are taken from the Holy Bible, New International Version, copyright © 1973, 1978, 1984 by International Bible Society, and are used by permission of Hodder & Stoughton Publishers, a member of the Hachette Livre Group UK. All rights reserved. 'NIV' is a registered trademark of International Bible Society. UK trademark number 1448790.

Scripture quotations taken from The Holy Bible, Today's New International Version. Copyright © 2004 by International Bible Society. Used by permission of Hodder & Stoughton Publishers, a member of the Hachette Livre Group UK. All rights reserved. 'TNIV' is a registered trademark of International Bible Society.

Scripture quotations from The New Revised Standard Version of the Bible, Anglicised Edition, copyright © 1989, 1995 by the Division of Christian Education of the National Council of the Churches of Christ in the United States of America, are used by permission. All rights reserved.

Scripture quotations from The Revised Standard Version of the Bible, copyright © 1946, 1952, 1971 by the Division of Christian Education of the National Council of the Churches of Christ in the United States of America, are used by permission. All rights reserved.

The paper used in the production of this publication was supplied by mills that source their raw materials from sustainably managed forests. Soy-based inks were used in its printing and the laminate film is biodegradable.

A catalogue record for this book is available from the British Library

Printed in Singapore by Craft Print International Ltd

Patrick Whitworth

Paul as Pastor

Biblical insights for pastoral ministry

For the congregation of Christ Church, Gipsy Hill,
All Saints Weston, St Martin's North Stoke
and St Mary's Langbridge,
whom I have had the privilege of pastoring.

*'For the guiding of man, the most variable and manifold
of creatures, seems to me in very deed to be the art of arts.'*
GREGORY OF NAZIANZUS,
FROM ORATION II IN DEFENCE OF HIS FLIGHT TO PONTUS

Preface

Paul strides like a colossus across the early years of Christianity. Described by one account as 'a man of small stature, with his eyebrows meeting and a rather large nose, somewhat baldheaded, bandylegged, strongly built, of gracious presence, for sometimes he looked like a man and sometimes he had the face of an Angel',[1] Paul is known principally as an evangelist and church planter. No one did more to take the good news of Christ to the communities of the Roman Empire in Asia and Europe in the years following the earthly life of Jesus, probably only missing out Spain, north Africa and northern Europe. But undergirding his extraordinary missionary journeys, with their drama, confrontation and fruitfulness, were both a unique teaching ministry and a passionate pastoral one. There have been innumerable books by authors far more qualified than I on Paul's theology and missiological practice but far fewer—if any currently in circulation—on Paul as pastor, yet he was the greatest pastor of the early churches, giving us a pattern for all subsequent pastoral care.

Pastoral care is the essential follow-on to mission and evangelism. It is also the necessary companion to a teaching ministry. If no attention is paid to the formation of Christ in an individual, family or community, then, little will remain of the results of evangelism as the tides of secularism, the world's powerful influences and the pressure to conform crash on the beachheads of our missionary landings. Equally, if teaching—however profound, correct or coherent—is given at a distance, it is unlikely to bring the support, help and change to the Christian who is struggling with all that she or he faces. Paul engaged in pastoral care in the context of close encounter, by impassioned letters and some painful meetings. He gives us the vocabulary of pastoral care: 'freedom', 'maturity' and 'formation'. He gives the objects of pastoral care: 'unity', 'purity' and 'community'. He gives us the trilogy of 'faith, hope and love', which would sustain churches in their discipleship. His own example, so often summed up by memorable one-liners (for example, 'For me to live is Christ and to die is gain'), serve as possibly the most powerful influence on those he cared for. His life was therefore a pastoral model as much as his teaching gives us a pastoral paradigm.

Much more could be said about his pastoral care than this brief book can encompass but, by spotting any such omission, perhaps those charged with pastoral care will find that their pastoral juices start flowing. Any omissions may stimulate readers to a still deeper appreciation of the range and extent of Paul's pastoral caring. Women and men are called to be pastors in the primary sense of tending the flock of God, whether in a specific office or not, and I have made this clear in the text.

Anyone writing on pastoral care, not least a pastor who in one way or another has been involved in it for nearly 40 years, only realises more acutely their own deficiencies. I have been privileged to pastor two parishes/benefices (that is the Anglican model) in Gipsy Hill, south-east London and now in Bath, and they have provided me with the context for learning pastoral care, a process that never ends. I have been stimulated by travelling to many of the places Paul visited to found churches: in 2008 to Ephesus and in 2009/11 to Jerusalem, Philippi, Thessalonica and Beroea (harder to find), with companions Tom Peryer, Paul Bright and Michael Fowler. Previously I have visited Athens and Corinth. To be in the place is always an inspiration for me and makes the text of scripture live.

I would like to thank BRF, and especially Naomi Starkey, for taking on this project, for saving me from innumerable infelicities and honing my thinking on sometimes deeply sensitive issues for the church today. I would like to thank Peter Price, my bishop, for graciously writing the foreword and my wife Olivia for putting up with frequent sorties to Room No 1 in our Church Centre, where the cogs of thought grind slowly and the words are hammered out on the keyboard. All the deficiencies of perception of Paul as pastor are wholly mine, but may I finally commend his vision of pastoral care, which he has so openly and honestly shared with us, to all pastors today.

Patrick Whitworth

Contents

Foreword 11

Part 1: The shaping of a pastor
   Chapter 1: The making of a pastor 14
   Chapter 2: A ministry of all the talents 30

Part 2: The task of the pastor
   Chapter 3: Right thinking 46
   Chapter 4: Right attitudes and lifestyle 61
   Chapter 5: Right relationships 78
   Chapter 6: Right leadership 93

Part 3: The tools of a pastor
   Chapter 7: Prayer 110
   Chapter 8: Strength and weakness 121
   Chapter 9: Word and sacraments 129
   Chapter 10: The pastor's heart 143
   Chapter 11: The pastor as mentor 156

Conclusion 164
Study guide 168
Appendix 1: A service of reconciliation
   and communion 177
Appendix 2: Mentoring 180
Bibliography 181
Notes 183

Foreword

In 1952 C.S. Lewis wrote to *The Times* making a plea that the two wings of the Church of England sink their differences and make common cause in what he called 'Deep Church'. This was to be a unity based on the ancient Creeds and Fathers, the scriptures and the sacraments. It was a call to the common roots of ministry, preaching, care of the sick and dying, and a renewed commitment to pastoral care. For the Anglican, the parameters of pastoral care are well set out in the Ordinal and, whenever I ordain ministers or priests, I say these words about their work: 'He or she must set the good shepherd always before them as a pattern of his calling, caring for the people committed to their charge, and joining with them in a common witness to the world.' Although this work is especially focused in the example of the minister, it is also the work of all the baptised people of God. And if the good shepherd is the supreme model for pastoral ministry, the apostle Paul shows how it might operate in practice in both churches and individuals.

Most writers on Paul concentrate on his missiology, his church planting evangelism or his extensive teaching about the nature of the gospel; few look at Paul as pastor. What this book does is to make you think of Paul as a supreme pastor, for Paul was very much a man of the heart, driven by a deep passion for people to become all that they might be in Christ. Patrick has given us a vision of pastoral care which arises not from any special therapeutic counselling skills but from Paul's deep desire that people should find freedom and maturity, realise their fullness in Christ and be equipped with understanding for all the intricacies of life and relationships. A pastor's life is demanding—sometimes deeply disappointing, beset by personal weakness—but it has also about it both extraordinary privilege and an intensely noble aim of changing lives, changing churches and, through that, changing communities.

I recommend this book to you if you have become a little jaded in the pastoral calling, to inspire fresh vision, or if you need fresh resources. It combines many biblical insights with sound pastoral reflection coming from over 30 years in pastoral ministry. It will be helpful for clergy and laity alike. It will take us closer to the intention of 'Deep Church' and the goal of Christ being formed in us, which was so close to Paul's heart.

The Rt Revd Peter Price
Bishop of Bath and Wells

Part 1

The shaping of a pastor

Chapter 1
The making of a pastor

When we think of Paul, we don't immediately think of him as a pastor. This may be because he seems too intellectual, too tempestuous at times, too fiery and too pioneering to fall into that category. It is true that he did not spend very long in one place, often having to move on to evangelise in new areas, but his heart was nonetheless deeply pastoral, as I hope we shall see. The fact is that Paul was too multifaceted in both background and ministry to be thought of in terms of a single function. Rather, we should think of him in at least five ways: as apostle, prophet, evangelist, pastor and teacher. Thinking of him as a pastor is, then, legitimate. Indeed, apart from the accounts of his church-planting journeys across Asia and Europe that we find in Acts, most of what he has left us is a record in the epistles of his teaching and his pastoral care of the churches he planted or cared for. You could say that his teaching was, in fact, the product of his pastoral care, which was itself a product of his pioneering and prophetic evangelism. More of that later, but first we must consider the making of this unlikely but passionate pastor.

Paul's early Jewish life

Paul came from Cilicia, one of the provinces of the Roman Empire, now in south-eastern Turkey. His home town, Tarsus, was north of Antioch. Antioch in turn was one of the great cities of the Roman Empire, along with Rome, Ephesus and Alexandria. Paul grew up as part of the Jewish community of

Tarsus, which he described as 'no mean city' (Acts 21:39, RSV). It had, for generations, been an important trading centre, lying close to the Mediterranean and on a natural geographical crossroads between trade routes north to the Black Sea, south to Antioch via the defile of the Cilician Gates through the Taurus Mountains, east to Persia and west to the principal cities of the province of Asia and the Aegean.[2] Tarsus had passed from Greek Seleucid rule to Roman rule following the victory of Pompey in the region in 64BC. So Paul grew up in a Romanised Greek colony like so many of the chief cities of the region, and in a prosperous trading city with a sizable Jewish community. As part of the Jewish Diaspora, he was probably acutely aware of his Jewish heritage. Like many scattered Jewish communities, the Diaspora at Tarsus was more self-consciously and conscientiously Jewish than many of the Judean Jews themselves.

We know that Paul knew and was proud of his Jewish ancestry (Philippians 3:5). He was a member of the tribe of Benjamin, one of the most favoured tribes in the history of Israel, ever since Jacob blessed his youngest son as 'a ravenous wolf' (Genesis 49:27), denoting the tribe's military prowess and courage. Paul's ancient tribal links were to the north of Judah, and his tribe of Benjamin shared the city of Jerusalem with the tribe of Judah as its capital. Paul's original name of Saul was derived from the most prestigious Benjaminite, King Saul, who was nevertheless abandoned as king by God as a punishment for his disobedience (1 Samuel 13:13–14). Saul, or Paul, would have grown up knowing two languages, Greek and Aramaic, and would later have become familiar with Hebrew, the textual language of the Jewish scriptures.

Despite this diverse upbringing in a Greco-Roman Jewish world and multicultural background, Paul was raised as a strict Jew. At some point in his boyhood, possibly as young as twelve, he was sent by his parents to Jerusalem for a more formal and still more Jewish education. Paul recalls this in his address to the crowd at the time of his arrest in Jerusalem, when he says, 'I am a Jew, born in Tarsus of Cilicia, but brought up in this city' (Acts 22:3a). He goes on to say, 'I studied under Gamaliel and was thoroughly trained in the law of our ancestors. I was just as zealous for God as any of you are today' (v. 3b).

This training would have qualified Paul as a Pharisee. As a Pharisee, he was a member of a religious grouping whose name literally meant 'the loyal ones'—the Hasidim—loyal to God, loyal to the Torah and loyal to the calling to be set apart from the Gentiles.

Jerusalem was the centre for rabbinic studies: 'From all corners of the world young Jews streamed to Jerusalem to sit at the feet of masters whose teaching resounded throughout Jewry'.[3] Jerusalem was an extraordinary place, so religious that we can barely conceive of such a city. The population at this time was around 25,000–30,000 ordinary people, a fraction of the size of Ephesus or Antioch, which were upward of 200,000 each, while Rome was the largest city of the ancient world, numbering about a million. However, in addition to this permanent population of around 30,000 in Jerusalem, there were about 18,000 priests and Levites, some of whom would move in or out of the city according to their duties. There were a further 6000 Pharisees and about 4000 Essenes, making a total potential population of 60,000 people in all. The Essenes were a monastic-like community based for the most part at Qumran by the Dead Sea, given over to ritual purity and intense study and copying of the Jewish scriptures. Their numbers included 'lay' members in Jerusalem, according to the Jewish historian Josephus. Half of the population of Jerusalem, therefore, were directly connected to the religious life of the city.

It was to such a city, teeming with religious life and worship, dominated by the great temple recently completed by Herod the Great, and occupied by Roman forces, that Paul came as an adolescent for the serious business of being instructed in the law by one of the greatest teachers of his day, Gamaliel.

The Pharisees were not a monochrome group of religious 'thought police', a sort of Stasi (the notorious East German Secret Service of the Communist years) of Jerusalem. They were a force for liberation, a movement of recall to the Jewish Law in order to define Jewishness and prove a point of resistance to the Romans. In the process, however, as Jesus made very plain, they distorted the Law and made it a severe taskmaster for the people. 'Woe to you,' said Jesus, 'teachers of the law and Pharisees, you hypocrites! You travel over land and sea to win a single convert, and when he becomes one, you make him twice as much a son of hell as you are' (Matthew 23:15). The Pharisaic agenda in the final years before the birth of Jesus and Paul was 'to purify Israel by summoning her to return to the true ancestral traditions; to restore Israel to her independent theocratic status; and to be, as a pressure group, in the vanguard of such movements by the study and practice of Torah'.[4] These movements of rabbinic study were not singular in their views, but in fact were divided along two main lines.

The two main Pharisaic schools in Jesus' time were those of Hillel and Shammai, who were the two leading rabbis of the day. The school of Shammai was traditionally credited with having a stricter interpretation of Torah, the Law, than

Hillel. Hillel took a softer line on permitting divorce, a less confrontational stance vis-a-vis Roman authority and a broader view of Jewish scriptures, arguing, for instance, for the inclusion of the book of Ecclesiastes.[5] Hillel's successor as leader of this branch of Pharisaism was Gamaliel, the teacher of Paul. Gamaliel is generally seen as having an air of pragmatism about his counsel, arising from his interjection at the trial of Peter and John in front of the Sanhedrin. His advice was admirably matter-of-fact and realistic. To a group of people bent on destroying this new sect of Christians at birth, he advised, 'Leave these men alone! Let them go! For if their purpose or activity is of human origin, it will fail. But if it is from God, you will not be able to stop these men; you will only find yourselves fighting against God' (Acts 5:38–39). His wise counsel prevailed and Peter and John were released, admittedly after a flogging. But within years there were innumerable Christians in Jerusalem, Judea and Antioch (see Acts 11:21).

Saul, or Paul, would have been known to Gamaliel, as the rabbinic schools were generally small enough for each member to be familiar to its leader. If the other rabbinic school was anything to go by, there would have been around 80 members. Often these schools were led by scribes who had undergone rigorous training themselves. Many of the Pharisees were also priests: 'The pupil would learn from their master in daily life as in the lecture room; their master's actions, even his gestures were closely watched and from them they drew guidance on ritual questions'.[6] We can imagine Paul as a young man, attentively observing both the characteristics and the teaching of his teacher; but maybe he found Gamaliel too ready to accommodate or give the benefit of the doubt to the teachings of this new people of 'the Way', which had arisen around the crucified Jesus, who, his followers now claimed, had risen from the dead. Rather than give it space to breathe, as Gamaliel had suggested to the Sanhedrin, and so see whether the new movement was of God or not, Paul was all for stamping it out. So when the court turned against Stephen (Acts 6:12–14) and called for his stoning, Paul was there, like a plain-clothes agent of the court, consenting to Stephen's death and ready to orchestrate a further movement of intimidation against this fledgling movement, with threats and violence.

Paul conducted a terror campaign against the church. Luke tells us in Acts that he dragged Christians from their homes and committed them to prison. Then, having conducted a campaign against the church in Jerusalem and Judea, he was determined to extend it to regions beyond, and so got authorisation from the high priest to arrest Christians further afield in Damascus (see Acts 8:3; 9:1–2). Later, in his own words before King Agrippa, he admitted, 'I too was convinced that I ought to do all that was possible to oppose the name of Jesus of Nazareth. And that is just what I did in Jerusalem. On the authority of the Chief Priests I put many of the saints in prison, and when they were put to death, I cast my vote against them. Many a time I went from one synagogue to another to have them punished, and I tried to force them to blaspheme. In my obsession [the Greek means literally 'raging fury'] against them, I even went to foreign cities to persecute them' (26:9–11). An obsession to oppose the followers of Jesus drove him to these lengths of persecution, fuelled by his belief that Jesus was not the Messiah. This was a view he held in common with most of the Jewish establishment (although there were some notable exceptions, such as Nicodemus).

Whether Paul ever saw or heard Jesus in Jerusalem, we

cannot be sure. He was probably of a similar age to Jesus—perhaps a little younger—but even if he were ten years younger, their paths might well have crossed in Jerusalem. The thought of Paul as a boy or adolescent seeing the final days of Jesus' life is a tempting one. Like so many of his fellow countrymen, Paul believed that the Messiah would come in strength and glory; Jesus did come in strength and glory, but it was a different kind of strength and glory from what Paul expected. Eventually, however, he came to recognise this new type of strength (in weakness) and this new type of glory (unfading), as we shall see in his pastoral ministry. So Paul wrote to the Corinthians that through the Spirit an unfading glory is given, since 'we, who with unveiled faces all reflect the Lord's glory, are being transformed into his likeness with ever-increasing glory, which comes from the Lord, who is the Spirit' (2 Corinthians 3:18). Likewise he famously came to recognise that weakness could be a source of strength, writing, 'I will boast all the more gladly about my weaknesses, so that Christ's power may rest on me. That is why, for Christ's sake, I delight in weaknesses, in insults, in hardships, in persecutions, in difficulties. For when I am weak, then I am strong' (12:9b–10).

The Jews were looking for a Messiah who arose from the ranks of the religious establishment: one who kept the law perfectly in the way that they did; one who obviously kept the sabbath according to their ways; one who fulfilled the laws of purity and ritual cleansing just as they did; one who was prepared to take up arms and lead a revolt against the Romans rather than resisting the way of armed rebellion. Instead they saw a man who persistently healed on the sabbath, who looked for a deeper cleansing of the heart and not just of hands, feet dishes or bowls, who called them 'blind guides' because they neglected the 'more important matters of the law' (see, for example, Mark 7:17–23; Matthew 23:23). The Pharisees, for the most part, took exception to Jesus' challenge and not least his association with the sinners and lowly people of his day (Luke 15:1). Then, worst of all, Jesus' life ended in degradation and humiliation, at their own doing and that of the Sanhedrin. He was crucified on a cross, which was the greatest stumbling-block to identifying him as the Messiah (see 1 Corinthians 1:23). For Jews, anyone who was 'hung on a tree' could only be cursed by God (Deuteronomy 21:23). Jesus was crucified, but of course we know that this curse was on account of human sin, borne on behalf of both Jew and Gentile.

Jesus managed to combine in hostility against him those who had been formerly enemies of each other, such as Herod and Pilate (Luke 23:12), the Pharisees and Sadducees, the priesthood of the temple and the scribes. Most of these regarded Jesus as an impostor, and his messiahship as being fatally flawed by one or more of the 'unorthodoxies' already mentioned. Paul was of that mind, too, but he was to change suddenly, completely and radically through the events on the road to Damascus.

Paul sees the light

When the Jewish state won more independence under the Hasmonean dynasty of high priests following the rebellion of Judas Maccabeus in 165BC, it also gained powerful patrons, not least the Romans themselves, who were the growing power in the Mediterranean in the second and first centuries BC. In 142BC, a letter was delivered by the Roman ambassador to Ptolemy VIII of Egypt, which concluded with the requirement that 'If any pestilent men have fled to you from their country [Judea], hand them over to Simon the High Priest that he may punish them according to their laws'. Granting this right of extradition to the high priesthood in Jerusalem was one way of currying favour with the Jewish leaders, with the hope of making Judea a more compliant state under eventual Roman rule. During those years, the power of the Selucids declined—the Selucids being the Greek power in the region, following the death of Alexander the Great and the disbursement of his empire among his generals. This meant that Roman protection turned into a stranglehold around Judea and, in time, the yoke of the Romans was to prove far heavier to the Judeans than that of the more enfeebled Seleucids. So it was under such an arrangement of extradition that Paul went north to Damascus with his letters of empowerment to arrest and bring to Jerusalem any who followed 'the Way'. He was, says Luke, 'breathing out murderous threats against the Lord's disciples' (Acts 9:1). His obsession or 'raging fury' was as strong and as lethal as ever.

The story of Paul's conversion on the road to Damascus is told briefly and significantly by Luke in Acts 9. The account has many of the common aspects of a divine call to service: the bright and blinding light; the voice from heaven; the falling to the ground; the address of Saul by name. But what is, of course, distinct is that it is Jesus himself who speaks to Paul as God, and it is Jesus against whom Paul is said to be conducting his fierce persecution. The fundamental conclusion for Paul from this close encounter was quite simply that Jesus was the Messiah. This was the cardinal point from which all else flowed.

Later, in the account that Paul himself gives of his conversion, he tells a little more about the encounter that he had with Jesus (Acts 22:6–18). To the question 'Who are you, Lord?' Jesus replied, 'I am Jesus of Nazareth, whom you are persecuting' (v. 8). And in his third account of his conversion, before King Agrippa, Paul elaborates further about the instructions that Jesus gave him during that encounter:

> 'Now get up and stand on your feet. I have appeared to you to appoint you as a servant and as a witness of what you have seen of me and what I will show you. I will rescue you from your own people and from the Gentiles. I am sending you to them to open their eyes and turn them from darkness to light, and from the power of Satan to God, so that they may receive forgiveness of sins and a place among those who are sanctified by faith in him.'
> (Acts 26:15–17)

That encounter on the road was the beginning of a chain of events in which Paul was led blind into Damascus, effectively humbled and dependent (Acts 9:8b). His sight was then restored through the prayers of a member of the Christian community, Ananias, whom Paul had come to arrest but now through whom he received back his sight, was baptised and received the Spirit. For three days prior to these events, Paul had been unable to see and had neither eaten nor drunk (v. 9). What must have been his thoughts during this time?

There can be little doubt that, for those three days, Paul's mind, emotions and spirit must have been engaged in reworking all his previous conclusions and presuppositions about the identity of Jesus, the significance of his death and the reality of the resurrection. More than that, he would have begun to rework his understanding of the purpose of the Law and the way Jesus' life, teaching and death were predicted in the writings of the prophets. Paul had to understand that Christ was the fulfilment of all that was promised, but that this fulfilment had come in a way that the Jews, by and large, had not expected. So at the end of Acts, speaking in front of Felix, the Roman governor at Caesarea, Paul stresses:

> 'I admit that I worship the God of our fathers as a follower of the Way, which they call a sect. I believe everything that agrees with the Law and that is written in the Prophets, and I have the same hope in God as these men [his Jewish accusers], that there will be a resurrection of both the righteous and the wicked.' (Acts 24:14–15)

Likewise, when speaking in front of King Agrippa over two years later, Paul said, 'I am saying nothing beyond what the prophets and Moses said would happen—that the Christ would suffer and, as the first to rise from the dead, would proclaim light to his own people and the Gentiles' (26:22–23).

What is clear from these personal defences of Paul is that he saw no discontinuity between the Law, the prophets and Jesus as the Christ; rather, Jesus was the fulfilment of all that had been promised by the patriarchs and through the Law and prophets. It was his task, given by Jesus himself on the Damascus road, to be a witness to the resurrection and to proclaim Jesus as Messiah to both Jew and Gentile. As such, he was called to be an apostle, evangelist, prophet and also a pastor and teacher of this faith. This extraordinarily taxing and demanding calling did not, in fact, begin fully for a further 15 years. First Paul went to Arabia and then returned to his home province of Cilicia and neighbouring Syria.

Paul following his conversion

We are able to sketch together a chronology of Paul's life from snippets of information given by Luke in Acts, as well as by Paul himself in some of his epistles.

Immediately after his conversion, Paul began preaching in the synagogues of Damascus. To the bewilderment and, we are told, the bafflement of the Jews, he began to prove from the scriptures that Jesus was the Christ (Acts 9:22). At some point, their bewilderment turned to anger and hostility and they sought to kill Paul, so his followers famously arranged for his escape by lowering him in a basket down the city walls (see also Paul's account of his escape in 2 Corinthians 11:31–33). Although the narrative in Acts supposes that he went straight to Jerusalem (see 9:26), Paul himself tells us otherwise in the letter to the Galatians. There he says that after his conversion he did not consult any man, nor did he go up to Jerusalem ' but I went immediately into Arabia and later returned to Damascus' (Galatians 1:16–17).

Why did he go to Arabia—which probably meant the deserts to the east of Damascus as far as present-day Iraq? Presumably, following his dramatic conversion, he needed time to complete a process of emotional, mental and spiritual reorientation before embarking on so unique a ministry and so demanding a life. Not only that, but during this sojourn in the wilderness God revealed to him the full meaning of the gospel. Paul is at pains to make clear to his detractors that he received the gospel not from any human being but directly from God, which gave his preaching and teaching special authority. 'I want you to know, brothers,' he tells the Galatians, 'that the gospel I preached is not something that man made up. I did not receive it from any man, nor was I taught it; rather, I received it by revelation from Jesus Christ' (1:11–12).

It was only after the initial three years of preaching in Damascus and then for more than two years in Arabia that he went up to confer with the apostles in Jerusalem, and that only briefly. He stayed there for 15 days, seeing only Peter and the Lord's brother, James (Galatians 1:18–19). Many in the church were understandably very suspicious of him and, indeed, frightened—wondering whether his conversion was genuine—but Barnabas the bridge-builder introduced him to the church and assured them of his genuine conversion. However, hostility to his preaching forced Paul's withdrawal to Tarsus and Cilicia, where he was to remain for around ten years. He did not return to Jerusalem for a further 14 years, and, for the most part of this period, he continued preaching and teaching in Syria and Cilicia. It was a period of ministry that preceded his missionary journeys and is completely unaccounted for in Acts.

Paul, in effect, returned to the area of his home province and the neighbouring province for at least ten years. It is easy to overlook this and, through a cursory reading of Acts, imagine that after the initial period of preparation and reorientation of his life in the deserts of Arabia, Paul quickly embarked on the missionary journeys recorded in Acts.

In fact, for around ten years he gained experience, presumably as an evangelist, in the towns and cities of his native Cilicia and neighbouring Syria, but the scriptures are quiet on the details. What we do know is that after the rapid growth of the church in Antioch, one of the chief cities of the empire, Barnabas recruited Paul as the leading pastor/teacher of that community. The eclectic nature of that church, with its mixture of Jew and Gentile (unlike the church in Jerusalem, which was for the most part Jewish), made it necessary to have a leader who could teach and lead in such a way as to blend the backgrounds of Jew and Gentile into a new united missionary congregation, capable of dynamic mission.

The church in Antioch had been founded on the back of the persecution of the church in Jerusalem and Judea.

After the persecution, we are told, men from Cyprus and Cyrene (north Africa) had scattered to Antioch, where they evangelised the Greeks in Antioch, and from this the church in Antioch began. We are told that 'a great number of people believed and turned to the Lord' (Acts 11:21). News of this explosion of Christians reached Jerusalem (the mother church) and Barnabas was sent down to Antioch as an encouraging and tactful emissary, to discern what kind of leadership was needed. Barnabas is given a delightful and endearing write-up by Luke in Acts, where he is described as a 'good man, full of the Holy Spirit [the requisite *sine qua non* of ministry in Acts] and faith' (11:24a). Barnabas recruited Paul by actually going to Tarsus, where Paul had been based or living, and bringing him down to Antioch. It is at this point that Paul re-enters the narrative of Acts. He was to stay in Antioch, teaching and leading the church, until, through a prophetic word, the Spirit told the leaders of the church there to 'set apart for me Barnabas and Saul for the work to which I have called them' (13:2). Paul was now to embark on the ministry that fully used his range of gifts and would build on all his background of Jewish ancestry, training and learning, as well as making use of his Roman citizenship.

Paul, the Roman citizen

It seems a contradiction in terms that Paul was both a Pharisee and a Roman citizen, for the Pharisees were like a religious resistance movement to the Romans in Palestine. Their adherence to Torah (the Law and specially the teaching of the Pentateuch) was a kind of badge of defiance against the empire through their profound assertion of Jewishness.[7] Just as Moses had grown up as a member of Pharaoh's household and court and used its education and training to lead the Israelites into freedom and the promised land, so Paul used his Roman citizenship to give him both opportunity in and contact with the Gentile world. Moses' education in Pharaoh's household and Paul's acquisition of Roman citizenship enabled them both to be familiar with the imperial culture of their day and well versed in the best disciplines of education then available. Although Paul's education was fundamentally Jewish, as we have seen, he must have been well aware of the reach of the Greek language, its concepts and meaning, as well as being versed in methods of Greek teaching involving logic, rhetoric and dialogue, later developed by the Romans. He was a man capable of moving between the Jewish and Greco/Roman world with ease and confidence because of his intellectual ability and social standing. But how did Paul come by his Roman citizenship?

As we know, Paul came from Tarsus, a city governed by Rome, and it is thought that his family had lived there for generations as part of the Jewish Diaspora. It is also generally thought that they gained hereditary Roman citizenship through supplying the Roman army with tents, explaining Paul's skill at tent-making and providing him with a livelihood wherever he stayed long enough to set up business. Roman citizenship was highly prized. In 69BC, for example, there were about 910,000 Roman citizens in the empire.[8] Citizens were created for various reasons: ennobling senior members of a provincial city, so making them part of the establishment of a Roman colony; rewarding those involved in local Roman colonial administration; honouring those who had served with distinction in the Roman army; or rewarding those who had supplied the Roman army over time (as did Paul's family).

Roman citizenship, noble Jewish ancestry, Pharisaic training and familiarity with the prevailing culture made Paul who and what he was. But all this was to be suffused with Christ. He was well aware of these powerful influences in his identity, speaking of them in various places (see Philippians 3:4b–6 on his Jewishness; Acts 17:28 on his knowledge of Greek poets and culture). As to his citizenship, he used its privileges sparingly. He rebuked the magistrates in Philippi for imprisoning him without a hearing (Acts 16:37), he appealed for immunity from a flogging when arrested in Jerusalem and rescued from the mob (22:25) and, lastly, he famously appealed to Caesar at his trial in Caesarea (25:11). The privileges of being a Roman citizen, apart from general kudos, were access to justice, a fair trial and, if necessary, death by a quick form of execution rather than by crucifixion. We do not know for what crime Paul was eventually arraigned in Rome and which law he was found guilty of breaking, but, after his execution, persecution of Christianity would continue in different phases for 250 years, until the time of Constantine.

Roman citizenship in God's providence took Paul to the heart of the empire to make known the faith there, although we know from the letter to the Romans that Christianity had already preceded his coming to Rome. It made the Gentile world more accessible to him and his message. It completed the picture of him as Jew, Christian and well-educated man, and made him the type of minister or servant of the gospel that he was. His background and gifting were unique, and this gifting is what we must now more fully explore.

Chapter 2
A ministry of all the talents

There can be no doubt that Paul was a multi-gifted man. It seems that he had most of the gifts in spades, whether spiritual gifts, specifically granted by the Holy Spirit, or natural ones by virtue of his birth and inheritance. It is Paul himself who gives us the most comprehensive lists of spiritual gifts in the New Testament (1 Corinthians 12; 14; Romans 12:3–8). He tells us that he spoke in tongues, healed people, delivered them from evil spirits, restored at least one person to life, had prophetic insight and had deep discernment in relation both to individuals and to churches and communities. He spoke with wisdom that was more than human. Add to these his natural talents, whether linguistic, intellectual or cultural, together with a formidable character well known for its passion, endurance, love and single-mindedness, and here was a uniquely equipped servant of Christ.

As well as listing spiritual gifts, Paul gives us the paradigm of the fivefold ministry so crucial to the healthy life and mission of the church in any generation (Ephesians 4:11–13), consisting of the work of apostle, prophet, evangelist, pastor and teacher. In this chapter we will consider what each of those ministries means and how Paul himself expressed them in his work, as well as how they relate to the work of ministry in the church today.

The fivefold ministry

The fivefold roles or skills of ministry, as defined by Paul, are necessary for the equipping, maturing and upbuilding of the people of God. The aim of ministry is to 'prepare God's people for works of service' so that they may attain 'unity of faith' and 'become mature, attaining to the whole measure of the fullness of Christ' (Ephesians 4:12–13). In this way the church is prepared for service, grows in unity and comes to maturity. All these gifts or ministries are part of the ascended Christ's gift to the church and must be present for the body of Christ to be properly equipped. Without their presence and combined operation, the church in any location will become lopsided or stunted, failing to become what it could be or should be.

Of the five gifts, two are especially well known (pastoring and teaching), and most of this book is concerned with the combination of the two. The other gifts are generally less well known today. The term 'apostle', though readily identified with the twelve apostles, is not so well understood as an ongoing ministry today, while the 'prophet' and 'evangelist' are often given little space in the church—even though, arguably, they have never been more needed. Even if they are not overlooked out of ignorance or fear, we can be adept at mutating them, so that evangelism (the announcement and explanation of the gospel) can get lost in the broader concept of 'mission', and prophecy can be subsumed in preaching (with which it was principally identified by the Reformers of the 16th century, as there was little experience of prophecy in the church at the time). Alternatively, prophecy may be identified only as a judgment on society for its injustice, as in the case of such towering modern-day prophets as Martin

Luther King and Nelson Mandela. The gifts of evangelism and prophecy are sometimes given temporary opportunity to shine, but usually then return to obscurity. In truth, however, without them the church will neither grow (evangelism) nor be fully encouraged and directed (prophecy).

Apostle

The first ministry named by Paul is that of being an apostle. The original apostles were those appointed by Jesus to be disciples, bearers of the message and bringers of the kingdom of God (Mark 3:14). By the time of the first Pentecost and the election of Matthias in place of Judas, the criteria for apostleship were more clearly defined. Apostles were those who had been with Jesus during his ministry, beginning with his baptism by John, and were witnesses to his resurrection (Acts 1:21–22). Paul was considered an apostle because he had met the risen Christ on the Damascus road. The twelve apostles (or at least some of them, as far as we know) became, through the inspiration of the Spirit, the leaders and teachers of the church, writing much of the New Testament and planting congregations. Their teaching and witness were the yardstick by which all teaching was later gauged, and formed the criteria by which material was selected for inclusion in the New Testament. The apostles appointed by Christ, including Paul himself, were a unique group of people whose ministry and life could not be repeated. At its heart, however, the apostolic ministry was based on the fact not only that they had been appointed by Jesus but that they had been given a ministry which was pioneering in spirit, potentially global in reach and ultimately defining of the church itself.

George W. Bush, who is well known for his mangling of words, apparently lamented the lack of French support for

US policies towards Iraq by saying that 'the trouble with the French is that they have no word for "entrepreneur" in their language'! Well, 'apostle' means 'entrepreneur'. An apostle's primary gifting is one of being a pioneer in missional work and church planting, a groundbreaker who strategises for future development and then gives oversight to growing churches. But it is not a role that gives anyone the right to laud it over other believers. I have come across too many self-appointed apostles in various parts of the world who turn themselves into spiritual potentates, demanding financial and material privileges, prestige and power. There are and have been too many such apostles, in whom meekness is overtaken by majestic illusions, self-forgetfulness by self-aggrandisement, and giving by acquisition.

Not so with Paul. In fact, some of the churches he led, especially the Corinthians, wanted more of the very things that Paul believed passionately were not in keeping with being an apostle. Paul never used his apostleship to improve his income. Quite the reverse, as he still worked with his own hands, tent-making, wherever he could. He never used his position as a reason for avoiding what was servant-like and he never let it cloud his thinking about himself, giving him airs or graces distinct from other Christians. He was both an apostle and a servant, and, in writing to the Corinthians, he explained on at least two occasions why he did not want to impose any charge upon them for his maintenance (see 1 Corinthians 9:1–18). Although he had every right to support as a true apostle, he waived it so as not to be a burden.

Again, in defending his apostleship to the Corinthians, he appealed to them to look beneath the surface and not be taken in by the easy rhetoric and impressive words or demeanour of the so-called 'super-apostles' in preference to his less impressive physical presence and less polished speech (2 Corinthians 10:7; 11:4–6). He pointed to his evident weakness as the foundational qualification of his apostleship, a theme that was vital to his understanding of his service. This weakness was made up of physical sufferings (see, for example, 1 Corinthians 4:9–12; 2 Corinthians 11: 23–29), human disparagement (with others looking down on him) and bodily infirmity (for example, his weak eyes, which may have been his 'thorn in the flesh': Galatians 4:14–15; 2 Corinthians 12:7)—issues to which we shall return. Far from these things being a disqualification, for Paul they were simply the means whereby he was made more dependent on the grace of God.

But there was one aspect of his apostleship upon which he was intractable, over which there was to be no compromise, and that was his authority as an apostle. Once again, it is in his correspondence with the Corinthians that this is most clearly highlighted. Authority had been given to him by Christ's own words of commission at and soon after his Damascus road encounter (see his description of that commission in Acts 22:14; 26:15–19). He had not taken it, nor had he wished for it. This authority, which Paul also calls his paternal care of the church (see 1 Corinthians 4:15: 'you do not have many fathers [in Christ]'), was uniquely his and he would not hand it over to any other, least of all the self-appointed 'super-apostles'. It was this authority, delegated by Paul to appointed leaders such as Timothy, that he was passionate to protect from encroachment by false teachers. Paul had a jealousy for his churches, like a protective parent seeking to hand over a virgin daughter to her spouse (2 Corinthians 11:2). He would not hand over his role or relinquish his authority to any other, least of all in accordance with some superficial request for a different kind of leader, more in keeping with the cultural aspirations of the Corinthians.

Paul's calling as an apostle gave him authority to preach and teach the gospel, explaining what it was and what it wasn't, what lifestyle was consistent with it and what wasn't. Although his apostleship was veiled in weakness and suffering, it was not diminished in any way by these things, because it was not dependent upon his own ability or competency but on Christ's gift of apostleship to him through the Spirit (2 Corinthians 3:5–6).

Prophet

The prophet, fundamentally, is someone who exposes and expresses the truth about a situation, a person, a society or a community. The truth is God's truth, his perspective on the reality of the situation under scrutiny. Often the prophetic function in the church community is to discern spiritual realities and then to communicate them to the individuals or community concerned.[9] The prophet must rightly grasp the mind of God through the inspiration of the Spirit and then boldly communicate it where necessary.

In the Old Testament, the role of the prophet was fundamental to the destiny of Israel. In many ways, prophets were God's early warning system to his people, either alerting them to danger ahead and how it might be avoided or bringing comfort and assurance of his love and final redemptive purpose. The great prophets of the Old Testament, Isaiah (whether identified as a single or three distinct prophets), Jeremiah and Ezekiel, had this function, as did the 'minor prophets' whose message was consistently that deliverance would follow faithfulness and that judgment would follow persistent disobedience. As Brueggemann has said, the function of the prophetic community or word was to reorientate the majority to the heartbeat of God, taking account of the excluded, the overlooked and the homeless in a deeply spiritual sense.[10] In his book *Prophetic Imagination*, Brueggemann put it as follows: 'The task of the prophetic ministry is to nurture, nourish, and evoke a consciousness and perception alternative to the consciousness and perception of the dominant culture around us'.[11] The prophetic message was both a judgment of the majority who had neglected justice, righteousness and obedience to God and an assurance that favour would follow repentance and obedience (see Micah 6:6–8; Hosea 6:6; 11:8–11).

Turning to the New Testament, we find that the function of prophecy was generally different, even if the manner of acquiring the prophetic words was similar. It is Paul himself who spells out the scope of the prophetic in the new community of the church. He puts it briefly: 'Those who prophesy speak to people for their strengthening, encouragement and comfort' (1 Corinthians 14:3, TNIV). Prophecy has come to have a more personal and less national significance in the life of the church. It is a Spirit-inspired utterance about a person or group of people, and this inspiration provides its basis in truth. Indeed, prophecy properly begins with listening to the voice of God through the mediation of the Spirit and sharing the outcome in an appropriate manner.

Was Paul a prophet? Did he possess a gift or spirit of prophecy? I believe so. If prophecy means understanding the divine mind for a particular person, situation, community or nation, then the range of prophecy can vary from an insight into a particular person's life (as Jesus had insight into the life of the woman at the well in John 4:17–19) to an understanding of the future of the world and humanity. It is clear that Paul had what we can only call prophetic insights in these respects.

Firstly, he had insight into the lives of others that came from prophetic discernment. He received a message, admittedly from an angel, that all those accompanying him on the boat to Rome that was shipwrecked at Malta would survive (Acts 27:24). He was also given the discernment to withstand the spiritual opposition of Elymas on the island of Cyprus (13:10). Although this form of prophecy was distinct from the great oracles of Isaiah or Jeremiah, it was not so dissimilar to the prophetic actions of Elijah or Elisha, who contended for the truth of God against the encroachments of Baal. The point is that the prophetic range covers a wide array of discernment of God's will, from the solemn warning of judgment to the assurance of salvation and comfort, to the revelation of God's plan in a specific instance.

The second type of prophetic insight that Paul had, which is on full display in the New Testament, was discernment of the life of a particular church. He had remarkable insight into the nature of the spiritual struggles in the churches he cared for. If the primary gifting of a New Testament prophet was to expose the reality of a spiritual situation in a way that led to strengthening, comfort or encouragement (1 Corinthians 14:3), then, with both the Galatian and the Corinthian churches in particular, Paul's insight into their predicaments was the essential prophetic precondition to his teaching of them.

Finally, Paul had a prophetic insight into the grand narrative of salvation, not least the final days of our world and the history of humanity. In particular, he displayed this insight to the Thessalonians, comforting them with the prophetic knowledge about the *parousia*—the end of all things. In this, Paul was forthtelling the plan of God without a specific chronological timetable but having a clear vision of the future that was the corollary and fulfilment of Jesus' redemptive work on earth. So he says to the Thessalonians, 'For the Lord himself will come down from heaven, with a loud command, with the voice of the archangel and with the trumpet call of God, and the dead in Christ will rise first' (1 Thessalonians 4:16). He does not give 'times and dates' but he does know and indicate the closing events of history. That surely comes from a prophetic insight into the mind of God.

Evangelist

Evangelists are those who communicate the gospel so that people respond by placing their faith in Christ. They proclaim the gospel in a way that is both faithful to the unchanging message and sensitive to the audience to whom they are speaking and the culture in which they are set. They are aware of the perspective that culture gives people but they seek to reorientate that perspective around a worldview that understands Jesus to be the ultimate message of God to the world, by whom humanity is both judged and saved.

Paul knew himself to be called to proclaim this gospel (or 'good news') to both Jew and Greek, to his own people and to the Gentiles. So he says to the Romans:

> I am obligated both to Greeks and non-Greeks, both to the wise and the foolish. That is why I am so eager to preach [literally, 'herald'] the gospel also to you who are at Rome. I am not ashamed of the gospel, because it is the power of God for the salvation of everyone who believes: first for the Jew, then for the Gentile. For in the gospel a righteousness

> from God is revealed, a righteousness that is by faith from
> first to last. (Romans 1:14–17)

To this office of an evangelist Paul knew himself to be called; hence, later in the same epistle, he says, 'And how can [Jew and Gentile] hear without someone preaching to them? And how can they preach unless they are sent? As it is written, "How beautiful are the feet of those who bring good news!"' (10:14b–15). Knowing himself to be sent as an evangelist but also as a church planter—forming churches in the wake of his preaching—he preached with great sensitivity, understanding, passion and persuasiveness to both Jew and Gentile.

Paul preached first to the Jews in most of the towns or cities he visited, initially in their synagogues and thereafter wherever he could. His message was unvarying—simply that Jesus was the Messiah. His argument, which was most clearly and comprehensively made in the synagogue of Pisidian Antioch, in present-day southern Turkey, was that 'we tell you the good news: what God promised our fathers he has fulfilled to us, their children, by raising up Jesus' (Acts 13:32–33). In other words, God has remained faithful to his covenant to the patriarchs and has brought both forgiveness of sins and resurrection through Jesus. Having spoken of the unique calling of Israel (vv. 16–25) and the narrative of Jesus' life (vv. 26–31) Paul says that 'through [Jesus] everyone who believes [clearly a reference to the inclusion of the Gentiles] is justified from everything you could not be justified from by the law of Moses' (v. 39). Here was the implicit criticism of the Jews who looked for the law of Moses to do what it could not do. It could direct, teach and point to the holiness of God but it could not save or justify. Its scope was circumscribed, its salvific power limited by the moral weakness of humanity. It could condemn but it could not make righteous; only the gospel could do that. Paul's message at Antioch was at first heard quietly, but the wide-ranging interest in his message provoked jealousy from the Jews, which turned to noisy abuse. Paul then, as so often, began preaching to the Gentiles.

Taking the gospel to the Gentiles was part of Paul's vocation. God had said to Ananias, 'This man is my chosen instrument to carry my name before the Gentiles and their kings and before the people of Israel' (Acts 9:15). Likewise, Paul himself told the Galatians that the leaders of the church in Jerusalem recognised 'that I had been entrusted with the task of preaching the gospel to the Gentiles, just as Peter had been to the Jews' (Galatians 2:7).

The most famous example of Paul's preaching to the Gentiles was his speech to the Areopagus (Acts 17:22–31). This address took place in the heart of pagan Athens, in the open air, before a sophisticated and discerning audience who were well versed in Greek philosophy. Paul's words resonate down the ages, still speaking today to a European culture formed by the classical tradition of the Greeks, and demonstrating something more profound, more truth-laden, more truly transforming than that culture could offer. His address is a model of how to approach a pagan audience that is vaguely religious but wedded to speculative ideas rather than to a revealed understanding of the world (17:21). Paul begins where they are, quoting an inscription he has found on an altar 'to an unknown God' and some lines written by one of their own poets. Having started with their own perceptions or questions, he then proclaims the greatness and grandeur of God, who, by virtue of being the creator, cannot logically be confused with creation itself and worshipped as a part of it, whether as stone, sun, tree, stars or whatever. If so great, he cannot live in human temples or buildings, but he is also among us—indeed, not far from us—and can be sought and found. In a few words, Paul has described God in both his transcendence and immanence.

Having challenged the Athenians' view of God, Paul then announces that one day God will judge humanity and has set a day by raising Christ from the dead. The contrast with his speech at Pisidian Antioch is clear: there he spoke of God's promises to the Jewish nation; at Athens he speaks of God's purpose in creation. At Antioch he spoke about misunderstandings about the law; in Athens about a flawed understanding of God. At Antioch he tells the story of Christ's redemptive sufferings and rejection; at Athens he focuses on the proof of God's power and intention by the resurrection. The simple lesson is that Paul uses different content, style and emphasis with his very different audiences. It is an object lesson in how to preach, especially as an evangelist.

Most of us in church leadership usually speak to the faithful, week by week by week, but in a society such as Britain, where the numbers in churches continue to shrink, we must come out of our places of worship to the 'marketplaces' of our society—the cafés, pubs, sports clubs, local meeting places and, yes, the worldwide web. Like Paul, we must begin with the inscriptions, the song writers, the poets and artists, the national and global events of our age, and build the themes of the gospel upon them. In that way, and only in that way, we will be following in the footsteps of that great evangelist and church planter.

Pastor and teacher

We will take these last two ministries together—but not because they always exist together. There are many pastors who are not teachers and many teachers who are poor pastors. Paul was both. He was a teacher to his fingertips, even if, as Peter complained, his teaching was sometimes hard to understand (2 Peter 3:16). And, as we shall see, he was a consummate pastor, though not of the 'more tea, vicar' kind, the benevolent sort of English rector who might appear in one of Jane Austen's novels. You would be a little wary of a pastoral visit from the apostle Paul; but, for sheer truth, inspiration and insight, you would not find a more energising and envisioning pastoral talent than his.

Paul's teaching is laid out in the New Testament—most of which he wrote, along with John and Luke. It is he who explains the nature of the gospel as distinct from Judaism, taking infinite pains, especially in the letter to the Romans, to do so. It is he who describes the effect of the new birth and the working of the Spirit both in the individual Christian and in the community of the church—a Spirit who gifts the church with grace and enables its members to live together in harmony, despite differences of culture and ethnicity. It is he who gives a vision of the church as an example of the Spirit's variegated grace, speaking to both earth and heaven. And it is he who holds out the lifestyle to which the Christian is called in baptism, distinctly different from the pagan way of life, at the core of which is a call to a set of attitudes that resemble those of Christ. Paul was a teacher of the faith in a way that has never been equalled, however difficult some of his ideas may be.

Although he is acknowledged as a supreme teacher with great intellectual and spiritual power, as a remarkable evangelist and church planter with extraordinary missionary energy, and as an undoubted apostle and occasional prophet in the ways described, Paul is often overlooked as a pastor. This may simply be because the other roles were so strong in him that the pastoral function of his ministry is overwhelmed by the sheer scale and greatness of the other ministries. None the less, pastor he was—and you could argue that, without this pastoral care, his missionary energy and church-planting success would have disappeared like writing in the sand. Much of the New Testament, in terms of his own writings, bears witness to this claim. His reason for writing to, say, the Corinthians, the Galatians and the Colossians was pastoral: in these letters he confronted misguided thinking, misapprehensions, misconduct and mistaken belief. Likewise, his letters to the Philippians, Ephesians, Thessalonians and Timothy were pastoral: they gave encouragement, pleas for unity, advice and fresh cause for hope. The letter to the Romans is particularly a setting forth of the gospel, with Paul in teaching mode *par excellence*, though with pastoral reasons, too—bringing unity to a mixed Jewish–Gentile community and introducing himself to the church in Rome. What an introduction!

If the aim of pastoral care is to bring maturity and freedom to fellow Christians while enabling them to face the challenges of life and faith, and helping them become what they were intended to be, then Paul admirably displayed and fulfilled this aim in both his written ministry and his presence among these churches. He was not your usual pastor, staying for ten or more years in one place, but pastor he was, and now we must see what it meant for him and what it teaches us about being a pastor today.

Part 2

The task of the pastor

Chapter 3
Right thinking

It is interesting to ask what the chief function of a pastor is. On reflection, it seems to be a multi-tasking role. A pastor is not merely or primarily a counsellor, although she or he may have skills as a counsellor. Nor is a pastor merely a skilled social engineer, although it helps to know what makes a community work well and to put those values into practice. Values such as consistency, trustworthiness, genuineness, generosity, attentiveness in listening, gentleness and empathy all make for good pastoring. The metaphor that Jesus himself used to describe the role of pastor, which had been previously used in Israel of leaders (as distinct from prophets), was that of the shepherd. A shepherd leads, protects, feeds and nurtures, which are all functions of a pastor (see John 10). But the core of pastoring must be to enable a person to become a fully mature disciple of Jesus.

I say 'enable' because for a person to become fully mature on their own is beyond the realm of human possibility. It can only be done in community, with the aid of the Spirit, using the varied gifts present in the body of Christ, as well as word and sacrament. These are the tools of the pastor, which we shall consider later. For the next few chapters, we shall look at the scope of pastoring—the goal it is seeking to achieve, the target it is trying to hit. This may seem very unscientific or haphazard, because human life does not run in straight lines and is not a neat cycle of cause and effect; it is very often messy, broken and seemingly random. Having said that, there are two pastoral goals that are especially obvious in Paul's letters—a healthy understanding of the gospel and a healthy lifestyle that results from it—and the two are intimately linked. In this chapter we shall explore what it meant for the communities that Paul served to have a healthy understanding of the gospel, and the false understanding that he had to confront.

Getting the right understanding

Paul had to deal with three thought-structures, prevalent in the Jewish/pagan world in which he ministered, which threatened the formation of healthy Christian communities. Two of them, as we shall see, were precise opposites and the third was an unhealthy tendency related to a growing interest in Gnosticism. We could give them their common names of legalism, anti-nomianism (*nomos* being the Greek word for 'law', this means the opposite of legalism—being opposed to the value of adhering to moral law) and, thirdly, counterfeit spirituality. Paul deals with these three issues in his letters to the Galatians, Romans and Colossians (and also, to a small extent, Philippians and Timothy).

At this point it is worth saying, however obvious it may seem, that Paul knew that, for healthy Christian communities to display the grace of God as well as the attractiveness of the gospel, their faith must be founded on a right understanding of that gospel. Otherwise they would soon become lopsided, misleading or downright wrong in their demonstration of Christian living. As communities, they would not offer the freedom and acceptance that come from the gospel, but would simply reimpose another set of rules or obligations upon people or give them false ideas about Christian freedom or proper religious observance. These communities would never be truly free and they would never become fully mature.

Legalism

Anyone reading about the life of the early church as told in the Acts of the Apostles or the epistles will know that the greatest issue to confront the church at the time was the Jewish–Gentile divide and, not least, issues to do with the core practices of Judaism: the practice of circumcision, the observance of the sabbath and adherence to the Law. How many, if any, of these issues was the church to observe? How much of the Law were they to keep and to what extent were both Jew and Gentile converts free from the Law? These were burning questions wherever Jew and Gentile found themselves in the same church. They constituted the main business of the Council of Jerusalem, which gave guidance as to what was expected of new converts to the church.

The Council decided that 'Gentile believers in Antioch, Syria and Cilicia' should 'abstain from food sacrificed to idols, from blood, from the meat of strangled animals and from sexual immorality' (Acts 15:23, 29). Even this judgment was provisional, however: later on, Paul was to express the idea that those with strong consciences could eat meat that had been offered to idols, and food laws were to change further. Blood is not off the menu for Christians today (think of black pudding); nor is meat from animals that have been shot or strangled and not butchered, from the chicken in the backyard to the pheasant bagged in the countryside. Only the sexual codes of the Jewish law were carried forward and they are under fresh scrutiny today.

Paul was confronted in some of the churches he founded by a concerted attempt to take Gentile converts back to

Judaism, imposing on them observance of the Jewish Law beyond the moral commandments. It was this attempted movement back to Judaism that precipitated his white-hot response in the epistle to the Galatians. Why were they deserting the gospel of grace through which they had received the Spirit (see Galatians 3:2, 5)? Why were they going back to the law when they had received blessing, forgiveness and new life through faith in God's promise in Christ (v. 8)? Why were they seeking to reimpose Jewish Law upon themselves, thus endangering the freedom from the Law that they had received (5:1)? These were the questions that Paul fired at them as an apostle and teacher, but also as a pastor.

Likewise, in the letter to the Romans he taught the church about their freedom from the Jewish Law. In some difficult chapters in the middle of the epistle, he proclaims the Christian's freedom from the Law—not the moral structures of the Ten Commandments, which remain as a guide to truly loving living, since love is the fulfilling of the law—but the sweep of Jewish Law including the observation of festivals, circumcision and laws governing community life. Paul argues that, in these areas and others, Christians have been discharged from the Law, freed from its judgment and demands, and now they 'serve in the new way of the Spirit, and not in the old way of the written code' (Romans 7:6b). Paul was determined, as both a pastor and a teacher, to make sure they did not reimpose a heavy burden on their backs that was quite unnecessary. He wanted them to know the true purpose of the Law, as a guide rather than as a means of gaining the approval of God, which would always prove to be a spiritual cul de sac.

Can you imagine what would have happened if Paul had acquiesced in the Judaisers' demands? The full panoply of Jewish regulations would have been readmitted to the church, and soon it would have become indistinguishable from Judaism, with Jesus relegated to the role of a prophet. Christ came to give us righteousness as a gift resulting from faith in his promise, and the Spirit to indwell the believer, not as a reward for observing or keeping the Law but as a vital gift resulting from faith (see Galatians 3:5).

Anti legalism

If the legalists or Judaisers in the New Testament wanted to establish their righteousness by observance of the Law and circumcision, the antinomians were the complete opposite. They argued that the Law was redundant: there was no further use for it, since we are justified by faith in response to God's grace. The Law, they thought, has been superseded by grace, and so, if we fall into sin, then grace will correspondingly increase. It was an attractive argument but specious, for it failed to take into account two points that Paul is at pains to make clear to the Roman church.

The first point was that genuine belief in Jesus leads to a dynamic change of attitude and heart in the Christian. In other words, the person is made new; they have new hopes, aspirations and ambitions, no longer set on self but on the kingdom of God. Paul puts this in terms of the slightly difficult phrase 'dead to sin' (see Romans 6:2). The precise meaning of the phrase is hard to pinpoint. It would be unrealistic to say that the Christian is dead to the attractions of sin; they can be still alluring, if not compelling. No, Paul is saying that the agenda of sin or self-pleasing is no longer the uppermost one in the Christian's mind and heart. Although not dead to the attraction of sin, the Christian is deadened to the agenda of sin; more than that, the desire to live a self-pleasing life will have been broken in the action of believing and becoming a ' a new creation'. Paul puts it graphically when he says that 'the old nature', with all its old aspirations, was crucified with Christ on the cross (6:6)

The point is well made by an illustration that has been used many times before but still works. The difference between our old selves and our new ones as Christians is like the contrast between a pig and a sheep. If the pig falls into a muddy ditch, it enjoys the mud and rolls in it, feeling none the worse for the experience; but if a sheep falls into the ditch, it scrambles out as soon as it can. The Christian is like the sheep: we are no longer pigs yearning for the mud and ditch! We do not wallow in sin so that grace may abound, because we have changed and seek now to please the one who has redeemed us. As Augustine apparently said, 'Love God and do what you like', knowing that, through faith, our 'likes' have changed.

The second point that Paul would make to the anti-legalist is that we must rightly understand the role of the Law. Its purpose is limited: it can condemn but it cannot save. It can detect or expose sin but it cannot redeem. In itself, it is good and right and just, but it is weakened in its effectiveness by human sin, as Paul argues in Romans 7:7–25. Speaking from his own experience, he says that he approves of the Law, but on his own he cannot fulfil it. Only through the Spirit and through being made righteous by the gospel is Paul able to fulfil the demands of the Law (Romans 8:3). Nor will this be an automatic or perfect process, because there is an ongoing struggle between the flesh and the Spirit (vv. 5–8). The Law acts as a guide to how to live, within the context of remembering that real love is the fulfilling of the Law (see Romans 13:8–10, especially v. 10). The place of Law is not as a means to justification, which it is powerless to achieve, but as a guide to good living.

If Paul had not corrected these two misunderstandings, the church would have become mired in licence or law and may never have risen. Anti-legalism was an attractive concept—it was cheap grace *par excellence*—but it was fatally flawed. From such wrong attitudes Paul the pastor could not walk away: he had to engage his teaching gift and show both right thinking and a true path to maturity, but the motive for this painful process was his deeply pastoral heart.

Counterfeit spirituality

The third set of beliefs and practices that Paul had to oppose was found at the town of Colossae, one of the Roman colonies of Asia, not far from Laodicea, one of the seven churches addressed in Revelation 2—3. It appears that a particular false teaching or heresy had become rooted in Colossae and was threatening the church. If the Judaisers or legalists of Galatia wished to add the ceremonies and customs of Jewish Law to Christianity and the anti-law party promoted disregard of the Law so that grace would increase, the peddlers of false teaching at Colossae wanted Christians to add various spiritual observances to their lives in order to develop true discipleship. Paul touches on these observances in the course of his letter to the Colossians: the need for a special diet, for the observation of new moon festivals or special sabbaths, the worship of angels, the approval of regulations about clean and unclean objects, and the harsh treatment of the body (see 2:16–23). All of these had the appearance of wisdom (v. 23), seeming to promote humility, but they were unnecessary. When a voluntary self-discipline passes to becoming an obligation on the whole community (either explicitly approved or tacitly implied), then the very basis of salvation is threatened. If Archbishop William Temple was right in saying that 'the only thing we can contribute to our own salvation is the sin from which we need to be redeemed', then the danger of any or all of these observances is in the impression they give that we are more acceptable to God on account of them.

Paul is at pains to show in the more doctrinal sections of this epistle that Jesus, who is Lord of both creation and the Church (see 1:15–20), has done everything necessary to reconcile his people fully to himself; nothing more is needed but faith in him. Indeed, you could say from this defence, as in Paul's defence of true faith against the Judaisers and the anti-legalists, that all his pleas for right thinking are, in the end, a plea for a proper understanding and consequent practice of justification by faith. These three 'attacks' upon the church are ultimately an attack upon the right perception and proper outworking of this most fundamental part of Paul's teachings—that we are justified (put right with God) by faith in his promise to us, a promise based upon the complete redemptive and sacrificial work of Christ (see Romans 3:21–31).

The danger to the Colossians of this heresy was that it had the appearance of wisdom and greater holiness. In the same way, being a monk in the desert of fourth-century Egypt, fighting the mind-games of the devil, might seem holier than being a 21st-century conscientious father, doing the ironing for the family after a day in the office. Paul's point is that, since both people are put right only by Jesus' sacrifice, we should not view one as more pleasing to God than another. Their activities may result from different vocations, but this does not make one 'better' than the other. Paul states that such ascetic practices give the appearance of humility but do not, of themselves, have 'any value in restraining sensual indulgence' (2:23). Many of the monks in the Egyptian desert have said 'Amen' to that. Although far removed from society, their records show that their greatest battles were with lascivious thoughts, even though there were no external stimuli to suggest them but only rocks, ravens and religious exercises. Such is the power of the human mind to generate its own temptations!

In his pastoral writings, then, Paul battles for the defence of justification by faith. He inveighed strongly against the legalists as well as the counterfeit spirituality teachers, whose additions (which were not only superfluous but undermined the sufficiency of what Jesus himself had done to put us right with God) threatened the fabric of true faith. These additions only proved to be, in reality, very real subtractions.

In these ways Paul fought for right understanding and right thinking, and, in so doing, he shows the premium that he placed on the mind and its task in directing both faith and practice. The mind must be transformed so that a Christian may be able to test and approve God's will (Romans 12:2). As Paul says earlier in Romans, 'Those who live according to the sinful nature have their minds set on what that nature desires; but those who live in accordance with the Spirit have their minds set on what the Spirit desires. The mind of sinful man is death, but the mind controlled by the Spirit is life and peace' (8:5–6). Right understanding and a mind submissive to and controlled by the Spirit are his objective, and this was the ultimate aim of his teaching and pastoral ministry. The outcome of a proper understanding of justification by faith through God's grace (and Martin Luther said that any church could be deemed to be rising or falling by its grasp of this truth) should be both maturity and freedom, which are the goals of pastoral care.

Maturity and freedom

Complex and important concepts such as maturity and freedom beg further unpacking. What does it mean to be mature? Surely it is not simply the same as the passing of years, either in life generally or since coming to faith. And what does it mean to enjoy freedom? It must mean more than the absence of boundaries or restriction.

What is the essence of maturity? The answer has to do with gaining a proper grasp of four issues in particular:

- a deep understanding, both emotional and intellectual, of God's character—what he is really like.
- an appreciative understanding of his grace—how generous he is.
- a right understanding of the world around us, including human life and the paradox of both its beauty and its fallenness, its glory and its suffering.
- a right perception of ourselves, especially our vocation with its limitations, and how realistic we must be about our moral and spiritual weakness.

Life will knock us around, but grasping those four insights will help us gain maturity to deal with all of life's pitfalls and difficulties. Pastoral care will help towards developing a mature mental and emotional understanding of each of these four issues. This will take time and will also be part of the maturing process.

One person who has classified the path to maturity in recent years is James Fowler, a Christian psychologist.[12] Fowler marks out six stages of development, beginning with the innocent or intuitive stage—the early years of life, in which fantasy, stories, experiences and imagery combine in a seamless world of thought and imagination. The second stage is that of the literalist, reflecting the views of a child around the age of six, which they also bring to bear on faith. They love the stories of the Bible and are fascinated by the details of them (for example, the size of Noah's ark); their image of God tend to be of a stern but loving parent. M. Scott Peck says that, in the United States, up to 20 per cent of the churchgoing population retain this basic outlook, which gives them security and clarity.[13]

The third stage is that of the loyalist, in which loyalty to the peer group is uppermost in faith terms. This is reflected in a strong commitment to the tenets of one's group or the opinions of a presiding leader. In this stage, the loyalist is surrounded by the 'values, beliefs and convictions of significant others',[14] and this group makes up the largest percentage of the churchgoing public.

The fourth stage comes when the unavoidable challenges of life cause people to question previous presuppositions or where an individual's character surfaces with more insistent personal requirements; this has been called the 'individuate-reflective stage'.

The fifth stage, the 'seer' or 'conjunctive stage', is tied to the growing awareness of our own mortality and the restrictions that life places on us, whether due to health problems, loss, unrealised dreams or missed opportunities. As Fowler says, this stage is brought on by 'having our noses rubbed in our own finitude'.[15]

The last stage is that of the saint, in which the self is removed from the focus of life. There appear to be two almost simultaneous changes needed in a person to bring this state about: the complete acceptance of the ultimate authority of God in all aspects of life, and the abnegation of the self, in which it is removed from being the chief focus of life. It is a state of being at once both accepting and truly altruistic, in which survival, security and significance are no longer central to existence; rather, the person is focused on 'accepting and doing the will of the Father', like Jesus in Gethsemane (Luke 22:42)

The strength of Fowler's analysis is that it not only reflects accurately the varying approaches to faith at different ages and stages of life, but it also links to the different stages of cognitive apprehension at various ages or stages of life. However, cognitive development does not necessarily link to spiritual maturity. For Paul, growth to maturity was not simply age-dependent but was focused on grasping those four issues relating to perceptions about God and ourselves, including, above all, God's grace towards us. To the Colossians he said, 'We proclaim [Christ], admonishing and teaching everyone with all wisdom, so that we may present everyone fully mature in Christ. To this end I strenuously contend with all the energy Christ so powerfully works in me' (1:28–29, TNIV). To the Galatians he wrote, 'My dear children, for whom I am again in the pains of childbirth until Christ is formed in you, how I wish I could be with you now and change my tone, because I am perplexed about you' (4:19–20). And to the Ephesians he says that their growth to maturity will result from the operation of all the ministries of apostle, prophet, evangelist, pastor and teacher in their lives (4:11, 13). For the Corinthians, much of Paul's teaching and pastoral input was directed at bringing maturity to their lives in relation to sexual relationships, marriage, giving, right attitudes to spiritual gifts and questions about what is truly wise or powerful—issues to which we will return.

If maturity was Paul's goal in pastoral care, it was to be found in the context of freedom. To Paul, freedom is possible only through a right understanding of grace, the operation of God's unmerited favour in our lives, freeing us from all condemnation. Freedom is to be the new habitat of the Christian, her natural territory, and yet often it remains more like a mirage or an oasis that we glimpse from afar without ever fully reaching. This can be because of a multitude of causes: low self-esteem or a sense of rejection from an unhappy childhood; addictions to powerful stimuli such as drugs, alcohol or pornography; an inability to trust because of disappointment in close relationships that should have been trustworthy but were not. All these things can make freedom hard—the freedom simply to be comfortable in our own skins, confident of God's love as we are and not wishing that we were something other than we were made to be.

For Paul, freedom existed as the flipside to accountability. He knew that he was not free to do whatever he liked, either morally or spiritually; he was free, rather, to become what he had been created to be, and that under the authority or Lordship of Christ (Romans 6:18; Galatians 5:13). Here was the essential paradox of freedom: we are most free when we are most fulfilled, and true fulfilment can only truly come from his service; so his service is perfect freedom (and the claim that to be a slave to Christ is to be perfectly free is, in fact, the truth). Since we were created to be completely fulfilled in a relationship with God, our freedom comes when that relationship is fulfilled, and it is fulfilled when we know his will for the pattern of our lives.

We should not think of God's will as being like a print-out

for life but, rather, as a developing relationship of dynamic trust in him. It is not a question of taking a wrong turn or making a wrong choice in, say, a career move or a house purchase and then finding that we have blown it! Rather, in each circumstance we have a pattern of life to follow and a new set of challenges to face, to prove the sufficiency of his grace which enables us to become more of what we were intended to be. I was recently being driven in a friend's car with a sophisticated and highly personal navigation system. Whenever we took a wrong turn, a voice declared, 'Wrong turning made'—but we were then re-routed from that point with the reassuring words 'New route to destination will take account of wrong turning and take remedial action.' In other words, mistakes did not mean we had to return to the beginning. Our new route would incorporate the mistake. This, too, is the way of freedom.

Paul wanted his churches to know and enjoy that kind of freedom, but several were in danger of selling out to legalism (the Galatians) or its opposite, antinomianism, or unnecessary religious practices (the Colossians). Thus they were in danger of passing up their freedom and entering into a new bondage or slavery. To the Corinthians he said, 'Where the Spirit of the Lord is, there is freedom' (2 Corinthians 3:17); to the Galatians he cried out, 'It is for freedom that Christ has set us free. Stand firm, then, and do not let yourselves be burdened again by a yoke of slavery' (5:1). He wanted them to be free and he wanted them to be mature and, to this end, as a pastor-teacher he had to remonstrate with their false ideas.

Today, the pastor-teacher may have to confront, however lovingly or diplomatically, ideas that threaten to eclipse the gospel, stunt development, cramp freedom or prevent maturation. The wrong thinking in question may be a confusion of the mission of the church with the upkeep of the church building, or it might be placing far more importance on ceremony than on content, or it might be rating right doctrine about secondary issues as far superior to relationships in terms of proclaiming the gospel. Paul placed a high premium on right thinking but he placed an equal importance on making right thinking visible through good relationships and lifestyle. Right thinking, for Paul, would always lead on to right attitudes and lifestyle; it was never a purely academic pursuit. There is no point in knowing the right answers if they never lead to a community that is brimming with the love of God.

Chapter 4
Right attitudes and lifestyle

If one of Paul's main concerns as a pastor was right thinking, his concern for right attitudes and lifestyle was of equal importance. In fact, most of his epistles progress from combating wrong ideas or false teaching, as well as putting forward right thinking or a truthful picture of God and ourselves, to a description of both the right attitudes we should have and the right lifestyle we should adopt. A pastor must concern herself with both forming right attitudes and encouraging a healthy and godly lifestyle among the people she leads. Like teaching, it must begin with the pastor himself, and that is, of course, a demanding challenge. The 18th-century missionary David Brainerd was once asked what was his people's greatest need. He replied, 'My holiness.' Likewise, when Jesus sat down to teach in the Sermon of the Mount, he began with a list of 'blessed attitudes' or beatitudes, the foundation of the spirituality and outlook that he wanted to see in his disciples. Holiness, to use Brainerd's answer, does not principally mean a sparing asceticism or obvious self-denial when it comes to the pleasures of life so much as the forming of those attitudes that are present in God himself: faithfulness, steadfast love, humility, generosity, graciousness and honesty, to name but a few. The presence of these qualities in the pastor's life will act as an example and spur to those he or she leads.

Paul clearly saw the formation of right attitudes as a primary task both in our personal discipleship and in pastoral care. Such attitudes were the product of right thinking about ourselves, about God's grace and in facing the struggles of life and faith. So what were the attitudes that Paul sought in the churches he led, and that he himself manifested?

Thankfulness

Paul himself remained remarkably thankful throughout his ministry, and nowhere is this more apparent than in his letter to the Philippians. Although imprisoned and awaiting trial and most probably execution, he writes of continual rejoicing in Christ: 'Rejoice in the Lord always. I will say it again: rejoice!' (4:4). He tells the Philippians always to accompany their prayers with thanksgiving. They should inhabit a habitat of praise and thanksgiving, whatever the challenge.

On Easter Day 2010, a friend from college days and distinguished Anglican minister of a central Cambridge church, Mark Ashton, died from cancer. He had been given only nine months to live from its diagnosis. Having received the news of untreatable cancer, he was still able to write:

> I have lived 62 years of very happy life on earth, and for over 40 years of them Jesus has been my Lord and Saviour. So I can have no regrets. My main reaction was then, and remains now, one of gratitude. God has done all things well, and I believe he is doing this thing well too. He is taking me back to himself when I have all my faculties, when I am still active in ministry, when my family have reached independence with their spouses and careers, and when my wife still has the energy and vitality to face a new stage of life.[16]

Also, in a YouTube clip made some months before, in which he was giving a talk to an assembled group, Mark spoke about the Christian faith, exuding gratitude, faith and confidence. His hope was not based on healing in this life, however marvellous that might be, but on the hope of heaven. To express such gratitude while facing separation from his wife and family was not only a work of grace but one of sheer determination and confidence in God's promises. Mark's ability to be grateful for the blessings of life right up to the moment of death was an inspiration that none who witnessed it or heard of it would forget.

Paul's writings, likewise, exuded gratitude—as he made clear repeatedly, for instance, to the Philippians (4:4)—and he encouraged all Christians to have this refreshing spirit of thankfulness as a basic disposition. If we do not have gratitude, it may be for countless reasons: a temperament that is predisposed to be gloomy; a weak grasp of the significance of God's promise to be with us in the challenges we face (see Jeremiah 1:8); a life that is caught between competing ambitions, one of which may be contrary to God's will; or a period of profound depression that clouds our whole perception of life. But however difficult it may be to hold on to gratitude, it was an attitude that Paul expected to find in the church, not only because of what Christians had been delivered from but because of what they had been promised in the future.

Humility

Another attitude that Paul expected to find in his churches was humility. Once again, the argument for the importance of this particular attitude may be most vividly found in his letter to the Philippians. There appears to have been a little rivalry among the church members and, in particular, between Euodia and Syntyche (4:2). Whatever the cause of their dissension, Paul saw the solution as following the example of Jesus who gave up the majesty of heaven and the privileges of the Godhead to become a servant, a human and, eventually, a sacrifice and victim on the cross (2:5–11). This meant taking the path of humility, which in turn meant 'Do nothing out of selfish ambition or vain conceit, but in humility consider others better than yourselves' (v. 3).

Again, it is an attitude that must come from the pastor himself or herself, and from there it should fill the church. As far as the pastor is concerned, humility will be expressed by a low-key view of their own importance, a willingness to laugh at themselves, occasionally being willing to share their own weaknesses or failings as appropriate and being attentive to people and their needs, as well as participating in ordinary tasks in the church such as moving chairs or taking part in work parties. The more the church can see this quality in their leader, the more they will make it an aspiration in their lives as well. Augustine of Hippo, in one of his sermons, wrote:

> Construct no other way for yourself of grasping and holding the truth than the way constructed by Him who, as God, saw how faltering our steps were. The way is first, humility, second, humility, third, humility, and however often you should ask me, I would say the same, not because there are no other precepts to be explained, but if humility does not precede and accompany and follow every good work we do, and if it is not set before us to look upon, and beside us to lean upon, and behind us to fence us in, pride will wrest from our hand any good we do while we are in the very act of taking pleasure in it.[17]

Humility is a right attitude for us to cultivate because it produces a realistic and sober estimate of ourselves as weak, susceptible and vulnerable people, thus preventing us from excessive self-confidence in the life or ministry to which we have been called.

Patient endurance

Another attitude that Paul expected to find in the church, and about which he wrote a good deal, is patient endurance or perseverance. Anyone who has been engaged in either church life or, indeed, living out their faith will not have done so for long without discovering the need for endurance or perseverance. This is not just because of the pitfalls or disagreements of church life itself (which are far too frequent) but because of the difficulty of making spiritual progress in the so-called developed world, which has become so antipathetic to the gospel. For Paul, the context for cultivating such endurance and perseverance was the opposition or persecution that the church may encounter in the world. In Romans 5, he outlines the consequences to the Christian of their justification— 'Since we have been justified through faith, we have peace with God' (v. 1)—and he goes on to describe the blessings of this status. We have access through prayer to God; we rejoice in the hope of glory; suffering (especially suffering that arises from persecution) will produce perseverance or endurance, and this in turn will generate hope. Nor will this hope prove a disappointment, because 'God has poured out his love into our hearts by the Holy Spirit' (v. 5). It is worth noting that this outpouring of God's love into our hearts is, in fact, in the midst of a situation of struggle.

Around the world there are many Christians who find their faith a target for persecution. They are among many others who, by virtue of opposing injustice and dictatorship, also face persecution, not least in Syria, other parts of the Middle East, Pakistan and Afghanistan today. Ironically, since the 'liberation' of Iraq by the West, many Christians have found themselves kidnapped, harassed or killed. The Anglican Vicar of Baghdad, Canon Andrew White, often reminds us in Britain that the death of Christians through persecution is an almost weekly occurrence there. Their community needs patient endurance in the face of extreme provocation and persecution. Likewise, Coptic Christians in Alexandria (which I visited recently) have found themselves to be the target of violent attack.

Although there is no such comparable persecution of Christians in Britain, nonetheless we may well find ourselves on the margins of society, or, as I have written elsewhere, 'in exile' in our own country.[18] One recent court judgment made it clear that Christians could not enjoy preferential treatment under the law when their view on moral questions conflicted with the application of the law. The effect of this ruling could prevent Christians from holding certain positions where such conflicts might arise. They may not be persecuted but they could be said to be marginalised.

While increasing marginalisation of Christians may occur in the future, endurance of a more everyday kind is, of course, important for pastor and congregation alike in the routine life of most churches. For instance, patience may be needed with a difficult colleague or a lengthy and convoluted process of change; you may need perseverance with a leadership team who do not see things in the way you do; or it may even be that you as the pastor need to change a wrongly held perception. Patient endurance is needed for the work of God to flourish; if the pastor or people give way to embittered attitudes, or disputes become personalised in any way, then the dangers of pastoral breakdown are magnified.

Gentleness

As well as patient endurance, gentleness is an essential attitude in church life. Most people would not call Paul a gentle character—passionate certainly, full-blooded for sure, but not gentle. Yet it is clear from his writings that Paul placed a premium on gentleness, both in the treatment of those who had strayed and repented (Galatians 6:1a) and in the way he recalled his own ministry among, say, the Thessalonians (1 Thessalonians 2:7).

In extolling the importance of gentleness to congregations and church leaders such as Timothy, Paul was following the example of Jesus. Paul had obviously not spent long periods of time with Jesus, unlike the other apostles, who had accompanied their Lord in his ministry from the river Jordan to Jerusalem and his crucifixion. Nevertheless, he knew well, from Old Testament prophecies and contemporary reports, that Jesus was gentle and humble of heart and, from him, followers would find 'rest' for their souls (Matthew 11:28–29). The prophet Isaiah, also quoted by Matthew, said of the Messiah, 'He will not quarrel or cry out; no one will hear his voice in the streets. A bruised reed he will not break, and a smouldering wick he will not snuff out, till he leads justice to victory.' (Matthew 12:19–20, quoting Isaiah 42:2–3). Likewise, Paul sought to bring gentleness both into his own ministry and into the attitudes that one Christian should have for another.

Paul conducted his ministry with gentleness. 'As apostles of Christ,' he wrote to the Thessalonians, 'we could have been a burden to you, but we were gentle among you, like a mother caring for her little children' (1 Thessalonians 2:6b–7). He went on to say, 'We loved you so much that we were delighted to share with you not only the gospel of God but our lives as well, because you had become so dear to us' (v. 8). To Timothy, Paul wrote that the Lord's servant 'must not quarrel; instead, he must be kind to everyone, able to teach, not resentful. Those who oppose him he must gently instruct, in the hope that God will grant them repentance leading them to a knowledge of the truth' (2 Timothy 2:24–25). And, of course, one of the gifts of the Spirit—and therefore one of the characteristics of Jesus himself—is gentleness (Galatians 5:23).

Although gentleness was an important ingredient both in the conduct of his pastoral ministry and in his congregational life, it did not mean that Paul passed over faults or wrong thinking, or was any less demanding of people in the light of the challenge of the gospel. There was never any likelihood of that, but the tone of his ministry—its default mode, if you like—was normally gentle, unless something far stronger became necessary. Why, then, is gentleness important? It reduces the possibility of resentment where people must be brought round to a different way of seeing things. Where personality becomes strong, it is possible that people will respond to its force alone rather than seeing the truth of a situation for themselves. Gentleness allows people to make up their own minds and take responsibility for their own decisions. It gives people space to move forward and to respond to God's voice themselves, not confusing it with any human demand. And if gentleness is a mark of the community, it will quite simply be a more restorative and encouraging community to belong to. So, as Paul said to the Philippians, 'Let your gentleness be evident to all' (4:5).

These attitudes of thankfulness, humility, patient endurance and gentleness are qualities to be found in the pastor and the pastored, and, the more they appear in the life of the pastor, the more they will probably abound in the lives of the pastored. They were qualities that Paul looked for in the lives of his congregations and, if they were not present, he provided deep theological reasoning for why they should be present. But if these four were some of the many attitudes that he sought to find, there were three in particular that could be described as Paul's trilogy for life. It is time to look at these.

Paul's trilogy for life

Anyone reading Paul's writings for the first time would be struck by his recurring emphasis on a trilogy of qualities: faith, hope and love. They appear famously at the end of 1 Corinthians 13, where, in extolling the supremacy of love, Paul says, 'Now these three remain: faith, hope and love. But the greatest of these is love' (v. 13). In writing to the Thessalonians he says, 'We continually remember before our God and Father your work produced by faith, your labour prompted by love, and your endurance inspired by hope in our Lord Jesus' (1 Thessalonians 1:3). Paul sees these qualities of faith, love and hope as underlying, motivational ones, which produce results of work, labour and endurance. At the same time, there is no doubt that, for him, these were the three key qualities of Christian living that he most wanted to inculcate in the churches.

Faith

More than any other New Testament writer, Paul was crystal clear about the primacy of faith. It is the basis of our

Christian lives, both at their inception and in their living. Fundamentally, faith means trusting or daring to believe the promises of God. For Paul, the supreme model of faith was Abraham, who 'believed God, and it was credited to him as righteousness' (Romans 4:3; see Genesis 15:6), and, in writing to the Galatians, he says that Abraham was the prototype of all believers: 'The scripture foresaw that God would justify the Gentiles by faith, and announced the gospel in advance to Abraham: "All nations will be blessed through you"' (Galatians 3:8). Faith is the necessary response to the grace of God; if grace brings the promise of forgiveness or justification, then faith is the only means of obtaining it. As Paul wrote to the Ephesians, 'For it is by grace you have been saved, through faith—and this not from yourselves, it is the gift of God' (Ephesians 2:8). Grace is the initiative of God; faith is the grace-inspired response of humankind (although that too, we are told, is a gift) and salvation is the outcome.

Faith is not only needed at the outset; it is also the only way to go on living—the food for the Christian journey without which that journey could not be undertaken. The Christian must go on trusting, go on believing, go on having faith. Faith is the essential attitude that undergirds all others, but, as Paul told both the Galatians and Corinthians, it will eventually be superseded by sight (Galatians 2:20 and 1 Corinthians 13:12). Here on earth we walk by faith, but one day we shall see God as he is and all will be disclosed. For now, though, faith is the air the Christian must breathe, which in turn produces hope, the God-given conviction about the future.

Hope

Hope is faith with the future in mind. As Paul describes hope, it is something that results from faith and from living in a world full of suffering and overshadowed by death. Paul puts hope at the centre of the results of being justified by faith. In the famous passage of Romans 5:1–5, where he lists those results of justification (being made right with God through faith in his promise), Paul says that as a result of that justifying faith 'we rejoice in the hope of the glory of God' (v. 2). And not only so, but the Christian may 'rejoice in… sufferings [most probably meaning persecutions], because we know that suffering produces perseverance [endurance]; perseverance, character; and character, hope. And hope does not disappoint us, because God has poured out his love into our hearts' (vv. 3–5).

The outcome of faith in the context of difficulty and suffering is a hope that shows itself in endurance and strong character. There have been few more inspiring examples of this than the hope given by the faith of one of the Chilean miners, Jose Henriques, who acted as a self-appointed pastor to the group of 33 men who found themselves trapped underground in 2010, especially in the first awful 17 days when they had no contact with the outside world. Twice a day he gathered the group of miners together for prayers, giving them strength to hope for their rescue and salvation.

We all need hope as humans, and to be deprived of it is to be cast down in gloom and even despair. The hope may be one of recovery after sickness or a major trauma, the hope of gaining a husband or wife, the hope of promotion at work or the hope of a fine day for a wedding. The optimist finds that these feelings or expectations come easily because of the way things have worked out in the past, or simply because of their temperament. The pessimist, on the other hand, does not assume that things will work out well, equally because the past has been often disappointing or because of a less sanguine temperament. By contrast, Christian hope is based on events that have already taken place, to which the Christian is connected by faith and which give an inward assurance about the future by the witness of the Spirit.

Hope, for the Christian, is therefore based on what Christ has done, and principally the resurrection. If the resurrection was not true, 'we are to be pitied more than all men' (1 Corinthians 15:19). Our hope will be vain, our message misleading and God's promises meaningless—because we will have nothing to offer against the shadow of death. But if Jesus has been raised, then the message of forgiveness from the cross is assured, Jesus is declared 'Son of God', our bodies will be transformed and redeemed, and our earthbound lives will have validity, accountability and purpose. Because of the resurrection, our life will be gathered up and completed in heaven, and the earth and our place on it will be remade.[19]

How does hope work? It enables the Christian to rise above the suffering of the world in the expectation of the outcome prefigured by Jesus in his resurrection. We need not say, with an oft-misquoted Henry Scott Holland, that 'death is nothing at all'. No, in the face of death we hope in the resurrection—something that has happened, which is already a part of and the harbinger of a new world order. Paul held to that hope absolutely, wanting to be part of it as soon as his work would allow him (see 2 Corinthians 5:1–5; Philippians 1:21–24), and he expected the churches to have the same hope and to live and work in the light of it (1 Thessalonians 4:13–18). However, hope is made all the more possible because God's love is poured out into our hearts: that experiential knowledge of his love in our hearts has the effect of maintaining hope.

Any pastor must deal with the reality of death, having a perspective that, on the one hand, does not minimise or make light of the devastating sense of loss that death brings, but, on the other, does not diminish the hope that rightfully belongs to the Christian in the face of death. Paul's pastoral response to bereavement combines these paradoxical attitudes: solidarity with the feelings of those who mourn, along with a hopeful expectation of all that God has promised and prepared for those who love him.

For Paul, therefore, sympathy marched hand in hand with hopeful expectation. He called for understanding and empathy for those who grieve, as well as sympathy for those who suffered on account of illness (Romans 12:15b; Philippians 2:25–26). At the same time, he did not see death as something entirely negative: for him, a death well borne was a powerful witness to Jesus and a sign of sacrificial discipleship. It would also, incidentally, be a release for him personally from the trials of ministry and provide an escape from the failures of a mortal and deteriorating body (see Philippians 1:22–24; 2 Corinthians 4:16b). So he was tender-hearted towards those who suffered but did not fear death himself. He lived at a time when the Christian community expected the imminent return of Christ, and this gave an urgency and intensity to life—not to opt out of it but to make the most of the opportunities it gave. This is especially clear in his teaching to the church at Thessalonica (1 Thessalonians 4:16–17).

Lastly, Paul's many brushes with death (Acts 14:19; 19:30; 2 Corinthians 6:4–10; 11:24–26) made him view it as a necessary part of ministry, through which he would enter the kingdom of God (Acts 14:22; Romans 8:17b). He was buoyed up in all these trials by hope, a hope that would not disappoint because it was supported by the pouring out of God's love by the Spirit (Romans 5:5).

Love

The third and final member of the trilogy is love, and, according to Paul, it is the greatest of the three because it is the quality that will abide long after both faith and hope are gone (1 Corinthians 13:13). In fact, love will last eternally as the basis for all our relationships. In probably the best-known chapter of all his writings, 1 Corinthians 13, Paul extols this virtue and explains what it is. The word for love that he uses is *agape*, which is distinct from the other three Greek words for love: they are *storge* (family love), *philia* (friendship) and *eros* (romantic and erotic love). Each has its place in human relationships but Paul speaks about *agape* as being love's supreme form—presumably because in heaven it will outlast the others. There will be no marriage and so no exclusivity in families, and friendship may be surpassed by the perfect expression of this *agape* love—but who can finally tell?

For Paul, there were two aspects to understanding this love: its apprehension and then its expression. To apprehend God's love was itself a spiritual journey. To the Ephesians he describes how it is necessary to do this with the help of others:

> I pray that you, being rooted and established in love, may have power, together with all the saints, to grasp how wide and long and high and deep is the love of Christ, and to know this love that surpasses knowledge—that you may be filled to the measure of all the fullness of God. (Ephesians 3:17b–19).

So great is this love that it can easily overwhelm our limited capacity to understand and feel it.

The 14th-century mystic Julian of Norwich wrote in *Revelations of Divine Love*:

> From the time I first had these revelations I often longed to know what our Lord meant. More than fifteen years later I was given in response a spiritual understanding.
>
> I was told: 'Do you want to know what our Lord meant in all this? Know it well—love was his meaning.
>
> Who showed it to you? Love.
>
> What did he show you? Love.
>
> Why did he show it to you? For love.
>
> Remain firm in this love and you will taste it ever more deeply.
>
> But you will never know anything else from it for ever and ever.'
>
> So I was taught that Love was what our Lord meant. And I saw with absolute certainty in this revelation and in all the rest, that before God made us he loved us, and that his love never slackened nor ever shall. In his love he has done all his works; in his love he has made all things for our benefit and in his love our life is everlasting.[20]

Like Paul, Julian of Norwich knew that revelation was needed to apprehend and comprehend divine love. If one half of the equation was a receiving and knowing of this divine love, the other half was in expressing it. Love of God and love of neighbour were the only possible response to knowing God's love in our lives. So Paul wishes to 'let no debt remain outstanding, except the continuing debt to love one another, for he who loves his fellow man has fulfilled the law' (Romans 13:8).

Apprehending this love and then expressing it in a practical way were at the centre of Paul's spirituality. He prayed that the churches he pastored would likewise know and express this love, and he often commented on the faith, hope and love that he saw in their fellowship (see, for example, 1 Thessalonians 1:3), since these were the foundational attitudes that he looked for.

Forming the foundations

A pastor must concern himself with the formation of such qualities in the community he leads, and this is often key to the growth of the church, since newcomers are quick to pick up on the prevailing atmosphere. Is there acceptance or judgment, trust or suspicion, warmth or coolness, harmony or discord, grumbling or gratefulness, hope or despondency, faith or uncertainty? The positive Christian qualities that we have identified in this chapter come from a proper understanding of the gospel. It may take both time and the crossing of some pain barriers to develop such an atmosphere in a community, and often the pastor's faith, hope, love, thankfulness, commitment to service and gentleness have a lot to do with it. But whatever stage we, as pastors, may have reached in displaying any or all of these qualities (and each of us is a work in progress), and however difficult are some of the challenges we face in personal life or ministry, our competency is from God. With him, where there is acknowledgment of our weakness and failings, all things are possible.

Lastly, these qualities should lead to a lifestyle that is healthy and holy, too. In his letters Paul spells out what this means. He talks often about the qualities that should characterise our relationships, such as compassion, kindness, humility, gentleness and patience, bearing with each other, forgiving each other and, of course, love (Colossians 3:12–14). He frequently makes clear the distinctiveness of the Christian community with regard to sexual relations, advocating chastity before marriage and fidelity within it, and repeatedly warns against any kind of promiscuity. He says that Christians are to work hard, as if they were working for the Lord himself, to avoid drunkenness, to be trustworthy and to speak graciously and honestly. And, as a good pastor, he explains what these things mean for day-to-day living, as lifestyle is worked out in the very practical business of being in a household, with each age and stage represented. This household living, with all the nitty-gritty aspects of human life, is what we must turn to now.

Chapter 5
Right relationships

The focus of Paul's pastoral care was the household. Here were to be found the relationships of husband and wife, parent and child, slave and employer or owner. Here, in the household, the intimacies of human life were to be ordered—sex and marriage, singleness and divorce, care and bereavement, employment and service. This was the place where doctrinal understanding and theological teaching had to be transformed into practice. The household was the economic and social unit of the larger tapestry of Roman life; and, since almost all households to whom Paul indirectly wrote were part of the Roman empire, they had a kind of commonality. How should they conduct themselves in relationship to the state? What were their obligations with regard to taxes and justice? How was sexuality to be ordered? What were the reciprocal responsibilities of husband and wife in marriage? How were children to be brought up? And how were relationships to be conducted according to the gospel in the extended family and social fabric of the household, especially in relation to slavery? All these questions had to be worked out in the household.

Marriage

There was widespread recognition of the importance of marriage for the health of society in the Roman empire, particularly during the reign of the emperor Augustus.[21] Engagement was seen as a binding agreement, the breaking of which was culpable in the courts; marriage was used to uphold the social hierarchy and was part of Roman social cohesion; some alliances were discouraged (such as between patrician and non-patrician families) but a 'good' marriage could advance a career. Divorce was hard to come by and had to be ratified in the courts.

Although many of these customs had to do with the division of property and rights of inheritance proceeding through legitimacy or adoption, the Roman understanding was that marriage provided the stability that a successful society needed; therefore, legislation should uphold it. The Jewish/Christian perspective, however, was that marriage was not only a relationship to be upheld by society through legislation but also an exclusive moral relationship in which two people committed themselves in body, mind and spirit to each other. This understanding proceeded from the moral commandments in the Decalogue (the Ten Commandments), particularly the seventh, 'You shall not commit adultery' (Exodus 20:14). This commandment (with its assumption of monogamy) was not often kept by the patriarchs—who, of course, pre-dated the Mosaic commandments by some 700 years—or, for that matter, by many of the kings of Israel (for instance, Solomon had a harem to match any of his contemporaries). Nonetheless, faithfulness in marriage remained a distinguishing feature of Jewish and then Christian teaching, and this involved sexual fidelity. By contrast, Roman marriage remained, by and large, a social rather than a sexual commitment.

As a Jew and Christian, Paul recognised the need for sexual faithfulness: the church had endorsed this at the Council of Jerusalem, when it enjoined on the Gentile converts standards of abstinence from 'sexual immorality' (see Acts 15:20), which, in Jewish understanding, had come to mean all sexual activity outside of marriage. Furthermore, he gave a pattern for marriage, which he explained most fully in his circulatory letter to the Ephesians and surrounding churches, and touched upon in his letter to the Corinthians (see Ephesians 5:21–33; 1 Corinthians 7:4). This pattern of marriage is founded and modelled on the relationship of Christ to the church, such that, just as Christ gave himself in love for the church, unifying himself with it, so the husband should give his life for his wife, unifying himself with her (loving her as his own body). In turn, the wife is called to submit herself to her husband in everything (Ephesians 5:24–28).

Building on the Old Testament concept of marriage, that a married couple become one flesh (see Genesis 2:24), the analogy of this union between husband and wife is the union between Christ and the church, which Paul says is a profound mystery (Ephesians 5:32). If the union between Christ and the church is a mystery, so likewise is the union between husband and wife. It cannot be fully described or the roles within it fully delineated, although some general parameters are given. The call to both husband and wife is principally to love. The husband is to love his wife as Christ loved the church—that is, sacrificially (vv. 25–27)—and the wife is to love her husband through respect and allegiance, submitting to him—that is, offering herself in love to him. Both make sacrifices.

The vital question is, then, what does it mean to 'submit', especially in relation to 'loving'? It is not easy to distinguish in practice between the two verbs. To submit means, surely, to give oneself up to someone freely and voluntarily, out of love. 'Thus love and submission are two aspects of the very same thing, which is that selfless self-giving which is the foundation of an enduring and growing marriage'.[22] Perhaps it would be better to ask the partners in the marriage service, 'Will you give yourself up for each other?', for that encompasses both loving and submitting, and the question could be posed equally to both husband and wife.

Mutuality is also a key value in marriage; indeed, most marriages proceed on this basis, and with good biblical support. As we have seen, Paul begins his teaching on marriage in Ephesians with the sentence, 'Submit to one another out of reverence for Christ' (5:21). (This verse should not be separated from the verses following, as it is in several translations of the Bible—for example, older versions of the NIV). It is a gospel principle that we find freedom in service and dignity in submission, as Christ himself voluntarily submitted himself to the Father. In Paul's first letter to the Corinthians, this mutual regard for each other is carried through to sexual practice in marriage: 'The wife's body does not belong to her alone but also to her husband. In the same way, the husband's body does not belong to him alone but also to his wife' (7:4). Indeed, any abstinence from sex in marriage must be by mutual consent, says Paul.

Mutuality, or sharing of decisions, work, responsibilities, possessions, bodies and life itself, lies at the heart of marriage. After 80 years of marriage, one of the oldest married couples in Britain was asked for the secret. The husband replied, 'That's easy. It's summed up by two words: "Yes, dear!"' That may not be a full-bodied exposition of mutuality in marriage but it is an indicator of the power and longevity of affectionate agreement and submission. For my part, after a mere 30 years of marriage, I can say that nothing has been decided without mutual agreement, and mutual agreement has never been impossible to find.

Sexuality

The average Roman household would have been quite lax when it came to sexual practice; slave girls were often used as prostitutes, and sexual fidelity in marriage would have been rare. As already mentioned, there was little concept of marriage as an exclusive union of body, mind and spirit with one person for life. Roman marriage was a legal entity in which heirs could be born or adopted and educated for the future of the family, creating stability, continuity and the possibility of excellence through education in the humanities, physical prowess and military or political service. Sexual commitment was not part of the equation for the average Roman, and nor had it been for the Greeks previously. Homosexual practice had been commonplace in Greek society, particularly in the early life of young males as they trained for war and athletics, and it was also connected to pagan worship, although perhaps a little less so in Roman life. Alexander the Great, though married to his wife Roxanne, still had a long-term homosexual partner, Hephaestion, who was of great significance in his life and career; in classical times there was nothing remarkable in such behaviour. If we understand this, we then see how the sexual ethic that Paul taught was in complete contrast with the sexual customs common in classical times.

Paul stood in the Jewish tradition of teaching and had an 'unyielding hostility'[23] to all forms of *porneia* or unlawful (that is, extramarital) sexual activity. For him, there was a clear link to be found in Jewish history and the Jewish scriptures between idolatry and sexual licence (see Numbers 25:1–3). Godlessness and covetousness were closely linked to sexual licence, and so he was opposed to the abuse of the gift of sexuality in relationships and practices for which it was not given.

The Corinthian church was far closer to the sexual practices of our own contemporary society than were other New Testament churches, with the dividing wall between the two communities, Christian and pagan, seemingly more porous in Corinth. There was one case of sexual misconduct not even found commonly among pagans, namely a person sleeping with his stepmother (1 Corinthians 5:1). Paul made a point of warning the Corinthian Christians to flee *porneia* (6:18). In many respects, their dilemma echoes the situation of our own day, where the church is constantly challenged by the sexual mores of society. The ready access to pornography offered by the internet, for example, has a corrosive effect on individuals as well as society at large. Once sex is divorced from loving relationships, then seeds of destructive behaviour are sown in them.

If Paul was adamant that no sign of *porneia* should exist in sexual relationships of any kind, he was also clear that homosexual practice was wrong. In his letter to the Romans he describes it as one of the results of a distorted worship of the creature rather than the creator (see Romans 1:21). However, the form of homosexuality that Paul had in his sights was the sort associated with pagan worship or the type of sexual practice, so common with the Greeks, of taking a young male lover in one's early 20s as a so-called 'purer' form of sex, associated with the gymnasium and the military, before later settling down with a wife to breed and produce legitimate heirs for the family and clan. What Paul would not have been so familiar with was a society in which a gay lifestyle had become a legal choice of sexual expression, in which even teenagers may deem themselves unalterably gay and believe that their sexual identity has been formed in childhood.

In society today, we see homosexual practice that results from a complex set of causes: it may simply be a desire for pleasure, it may arise from an orientation that is formed in childhood, it may arise later during the crisis of sexual identity that often occurs in teenage years, or it could emerge much later. The causes are varied, and the degree to which homosexuality can be said to be involuntary is still being debated.[24] Research has shown that, in antiquity, homosexuality did not arise only in military training (for example, at Sparta, Athens and Macedon), in the gymnasium, at the pagan temple, through exploitation or from the habit of taking a male partner as well as marrying later (as in the case of Alexander the Great). By later antiquity (for example, the fourth century AD), those who, by virtue of their own orientation, chose a same-sex partner were becoming more common. Whatever the cause and type of homosexuality, however, Paul would still have regarded it as wrong and not the sexual pattern for which humans were created. What he would have found striking is the degree to which it has become part of modern Western society.

The question that remains is whether such sexual behaviour may be acceptable if people are somehow 'wired' that way—through no choice of their own—than if they are making a free choice. Paul's answer would probably be that although the act is not what God intends, only God himself can know the measure of the struggle a gay person experiences in resisting the urges of his or her sexuality, or the measure of their responsibility in yielding to them. Needless to say, this is an area of great pastoral sensitivity where great hurt has been caused and continues to be caused. We must pastor, being mindful of the need to put the person's dignity first, listening to their stories and struggles rather than rushing to the implementation of principles that condemn. Instead, we must focus on building pastoral relationships on the foundation of love.

Singleness and divorce

Paul also had advice or commands for those who were single. For the most part, his advice was addressed to single women, whether virgins or widows, young or old, but it extended to young men too. It is worth noting that it was probably extremely rare for any single woman to live outside a household with a male head. Widows, for the most part, would live with male relatives and should therefore not be dependent on the church, especially the younger ones (see 1 Timothy 5:3–8). The normal social expression of a woman's being 'under authority' in Roman times was the wearing of a covering over her head (see 1 Corinthians 11:10), and to be without that head covering was to proclaim that she was sexually available or a prostitute, and without protection. Paul apparently envisaged that a woman would pass from being under the authority of her father, stepfather or uncle to being under the authority of her husband (if this is a correct interpretation of his teaching), and a head covering was a sign in worship of her being under authority (vv. 8–11). To a large extent, a woman's security in the world rested on such evident protection, as indeed it did in the West right up until the Industrial Revolution, and still does in some cultures around the world today.

For Paul, singleness was a vocation that only some could manage. If a person could not cope with living in a single state because of sexual temptation, Paul's view was that they should marry, so he wrote, 'Now to the unmarried and the widows I say: it is good for them to stay unmarried, as I am.

But if they cannot control themselves, they should marry, for it is better to marry than to burn with passion' (1 Corinthians 7:8–9). Likewise, his advice about younger widows was not to put them on a church list for support, since 'when their sensual desires overcome their dedication to Christ, they want to marry' (1 Timothy 5:11b). However, such was the crisis of the times for Christians, who were subject to persecution and, in Paul's mind, were also awaiting the imminent return of Christ, that those who were single should remain single (1 Corinthians 7:26–27, 31b). Interestingly, Paul's general rule was that a person should remain in the state in which they were converted, whether single, married or, indeed, in slavery. (We will discuss this further below.)

Paul's view was that divorce should be avoided. Christians were not to use the fact of an unbelieving partner as a reason for divorce, especially as Paul introduced the concept (presumably from the 'one flesh' teaching of marriage based on Genesis 2:24) that the unbelieving partner was 'consecrated' (made acceptable to God) by the believing spouse (1 Corinthians 7:12–14). In other words, so strong is the marriage bond in God's sight, and so strong are family ties, that the faith of a single believing partner or parent consecrates or makes holy not only the unbelieving partner but also their infant children (v. 14). Individual salvation does not undermine the ties of marriage and family—perhaps a more Jewish view of salvation than is often found in our more individualistic society, more sensitive to the covenant of marriage and the solidarity of family.

All in all, we get a realistic understanding from Paul of human sexuality, with his view that marriage is for the good ordering of this powerful and creative force. Paul does not wish to hide away the power of sex or suggest an unrealistic spirituality based on abstinence, which would creep into the church later through Augustine; rather, he offers a full-blooded acknowledgment of its power and presents careful advice about it, given the culture and conditions of his day .

For the pastor today, there must be equal care not only in the handling of sexual issues but also in supporting those who are single in the church community, whether bereaved, divorced or simply unmarried. Within the life of the church, each must be cared for, acknowledged and given the encouragement and opportunity they need. More than that, each may have a ministry made possible by their state: the widowed could provide valuable care and counsel, once the initial acute shock of bereavement has passed; the divorced could turn the pain of broken relationships into an ability to help others facing the complexities of marriage; and the unmarried often have energy and time to sustain many friendships, which can be mutually satisfying and enriching to others—not least to children, some of whom may be of special concern, such as godchildren. In a society where increasing numbers find themselves 'alone', the church can be a community where deeply held friendships may be found and nurtured. The pastor is the one who can help create the conditions where this may be so.

Authority and the household

Just as Paul profoundly extended the significance of marriage in the household from the pragmatic and legal institution that was Roman marriage to a form in which the position of the wife was greatly enhanced (by equating her with the Church for whom Jesus sacrificed himself), so he also both affirmed and clarified the notion of authority in the household and in the state. (Incidentally, it could be argued that Paul restored the wife's standing to the way it is portrayed in Proverbs 31, elevating it from the rather diminished view illustrated by the Jewish male's daily thanksgiving that he had not been created a 'woman, slave or Gentile'.) In terms of the household, authority was exercised in marriage, parent–child relationships, employer–employee or master–slave relationships and the relationship of the household with the state as a whole.

In most of these relationships, Paul assumed a basis of authority delegated from God to appointed rulers, just as Jesus expressed in his conversation with Pilate when he said, 'You would have no power over me if it were not given to you from above' (John 19:11a). This idea of delegated authority is expressed in terms of headship, which in turn is an expression of order. So authority is granted to government for the ordering of society, to praise the good and punish the evil. To rebel against authorities so implemented by God is to rebel against God (Romans 13:1–2). Likewise, in the household, children are to obey parents; equally, however, fathers are not to exasperate their children by an insensitive use of the authority they have over them (see Colossians 3:21). As mentioned earlier, husbands are given headship over their wives, as Christ is head over the church (1 Corinthians 11:3).

This pattern of delegated authority through both household and state was part of the Christian order of things, but it was an order or framework in which the wider principles of justice, love, compassion, mutuality and recognition were to be exercised responsibly. Failure to practise these principles, using an appeal to authority or headship as an excuse, would bring about strain and, in the worst cases, rebellion (in the case of relations with the state) or divorce (in the case of marriage). Authority had to be exercised in a way that was godly; otherwise the claim to authority would be challenged and sometimes resisted.

Sadly, the church down the centuries has been culpable for its repression of women and its intimidation and exploitation of children. In most of these cases, it has mistaken the existence of the pattern or 'order' discerned by Paul as grounds for repression or exploitation rather than as an order of delegated authority in which gospel ethics of love, justice and compassion are to be evidently and clearly at work. Perhaps this mistake was most clearly to be seen in the response of the Church to slavery.

Slavery

The Greek and Roman world, in common with most ancient civilisations, depended on slavery. (The Jews, who had themselves been slaves in Egypt, were permitted to have foreign slaves but were not permitted to make slaves of each other.) Slavery was 'simply the means of providing labour at the bottom end of the economic spectrum'.[25] Most slaves were taken from the ranks of the defeated enemies of Rome, but others were born into slavery. In Athens in the days of Herodotus (c.430BC), about 55,000 adult males owned between them 80,000–120,000 slaves.[26] In Rome, nearly half the population were slaves in the days of the emperor Augustus, and some historians calculate that there were as many as 60 million slaves throughout the Roman empire at that time.[27] Some 70 years before Augustus, when Spartacus rose against Rome, about 150,000 slaves took part in his rebellion, which was brutally suppressed, with 6000 crucified slaves being strung out along the Appian Way.[28]

Slavery was as much an institution in Roman society as

paganism itself, and only with the passing of the latter in the wake of Constantine's accession in AD306 did it begin to recede, although a measure of liberalisation towards slaves had begun in the first century AD. Even after 315, however, bishops continued to own slaves and concerted opposition to the slave trade on a principled basis did not fully come about until the movement for the abolition for slavery led by William Wilberforce in the 18th and 19th centuries.

Paul himself seems to have been ambivalent about the institution of slavery. In his correspondence with the Corinthians he is pragmatic: 'Were you a slave when you were called? Don't let it trouble you—although if you can gain your freedom, do so' (1 Corinthians 7:21). He goes on to give his reasons for this view—that a person's identity in Christ is more fundamental than his identity in the social structure of the world. In other words, our identity in Jesus is of more consequence than our social identity, be we slave or free. Hence Paul argues, 'He who was a slave when called by the Lord is the Lord's freedman; similarly, he who was a free man when he was called is Christ's slave' (v. 22). In his exquisite little letter to Philemon about the runaway slave, Onesimus, it is not clear whether Paul expects Philemon to free him or not.[29] What is clear, though, is that Paul expected the slave to be reconciled to Philemon as a 'brother in the Lord' (v. 16). Furthermore, his view was that Christian slaves were far from powerless, because through their good work and demeanour they could bring about change in the household.

While Paul firmly recognised the complete equality of all people before God and their equal worth and dignity (Galatians 3:28), he did not seem to feel that it was his role or calling to confront the evil of slavery head on, so ingrained was it in the economic and social fabric of Roman society. However, his hope was that the unity of Christian fellowship would in time dissolve the bonds of slavery and that his teaching about the unity, equality and dignity of all people would surmount economic arguments in the future. As history shows, this did eventually happen, but it took the best part of a further 1800 years; today, the 'Stop the Traffik' campaign reminds us that, in all too many parts of the world, the battle is far from won.

The pastoral challenge

Paul, as you would expect, did not shirk pastoral responsibility. He addressed in his own context a range of issues that were relevant in most households. It is for us to sift the unchanging gospel principles of relationship between husband and wife, parent and child, employer and employee and so on, and show how they should be demonstrated and expressed today.

The pastor today will find herself meeting pastoral issues that Paul would not have had to advise on. I have encountered all of the following, either directly or indirectly.

- How can we advise a family who already have four children on whether or not to abort a severely handicapped foetus in the early weeks of pregnancy?
- Can we encourage sperm or egg donation for infertile couples?
- May we take the funeral of someone who has taken their own life through assisted suicide?
- What about baptism of a child whose parents are not yet married?
- At what point does the demand for submission in marriage become a form of abuse?

- How do we help Christian parents when their teenage son or daughter reveals that they are gay?
- How should we confront the state when it pursues a policy of unjust aggression?

Some of these cases may seem easier than others, but they all serve to show the extent and complexity of a pastor's task—how resolutely, carefully and compassionately he must approach the issue raised or the need revealed, and how important it is to combine grace and truth in response to great pain, fear or confusion.

If that were not enough, the pastor is also to be the leader of the worshipping and missional community, which is the subject of our next chapter.

Chapter 6
Right leadership

Paul's pastoral leadership consisted in doctrinal teaching that was necessary for a healthy understanding of the faith, and instruction in the formation of attitudes that reflected the nature of God and a proper understanding of the gospel. At times, his pastoral care was provided through very robust teaching, albeit through letters, as in the case of the Galatians. This was not a question of tea and cucumber sandwiches and casual chat before the leader got round to raising his concerns. Paul came right to the point, as we can see when he upbraided the Galatians for slipping back into religious practices: 'You foolish Galatians!' he exclaimed in his letter to them. 'Who has bewitched you?' (3:1b). He could not leave unchecked false teaching or wrong living. The role of the pastor, as we have seen, is to foster right thinking about attitudes and a lifestyle that arises from right understanding—but for this to happen there needs to be appropriate leadership.

As already mentioned, the pastor can model, to some degree, the attitudes sought in his or her church. If the congregation see in their pastor these attitudes played out, albeit haltingly, the 'flock' is more likely to follow. Likewise, pastoring is about the fostering of good relationships: the pastor is encouraged to demonstrate patterns of relationships in his family that others can see and be encouraged by (see 1 Timothy 3:4). That, too, is a dauntingly high demand, and it may entail showing how to deal with failure as much as projecting apparent success. As pastors, we naturally fail and may be broken ourselves, so the example we offer is as much about how to go on after failure and how God is able to give fresh starts as it is about being paragons of family life.

This relationship between pastoral care and leadership may not exist in some churches, but it is certainly the case in the Anglican Church, where, from the moment of a leader's appointment, she is called to lead as well as pastor. What does this leadership involve?

Reconciliation

There is no doubt that a pastor is called to a ministry of reconciliation. Paul made this abundantly clear in his correspondence with the Corinthians. He had many misunderstandings or differences of opinion with them and worked hard to change their misconceptions about ministry and restore his relationship with them. In his second letter to them he wrote, 'All this is from God, who reconciled us to himself through Christ and gave us the ministry of reconciliation' (2 Corinthians 5:18). Reconciliation is needed in all kinds of ways—to reconcile interests in the congregation or, sometimes, to reconcile individuals who no longer see eye to eye.

The ease with which we handle conflict depends on the issues involved and whether or not we are directly involved in them. It is far harder if we are the reason or part of the reason for the conflict, as defensiveness and self-justification can creep in, and clarity of thought can become clouded by emotions. In such instances, it is best to have a third party to hear what each side has to say and to clarify the issues and how they can be resolved. Bringing people together may well be a long process in which trust in the pastor as mediator must be established and issues of conflict understood. Finally, if there is genuine grievance on either side, the parties must be willing to forgive each other if harmony is to be restored. In my own ministry I have found some kind of private service of reconciliation to be a useful tool and an effective way in enabling a new start (see Appendix 1).

A pastor is a point of reconciliation. A church member may come to him or her with a grievance about the way in which a service was led, the style of worship or the length of the sermon. People may raise a relatively trivial matter, such as the style of the new furniture for the church rooms. Questions arise, such as 'Should we go for cheaper furnishings and so release more money for overseas work, or choose more expensive furnishings that might be more welcoming to outsiders?' More seriously, the issue or conflict may be about the treatment of a member of the church staff or a volunteer. The matters will range from the truly large to the very small, and, in my own experience, barely a week goes by without an issue being raised that requires a thoughtful response and some form of reconciling ministry. Failure to respond can often lead to the situation being exacerbated. A trusted pastor who has shown concern for fairness and judicious treatment of people will be in an excellent position to exercise this ministry of reconciliation. The pastor can listen, assure the church member that they have been heard, promise to consider carefully all points of view and provide opportunities for change and healing.

We have been given a ministry of reconciliation, and it is a wonderful privilege, so let's use it in the interest of promoting harmony and unity in the body of Christ (see Ephesians 4:1–3). If we as pastors fail to engage as reconcilers, it is likely that disputes may come to divide our church.

The power of presence

In a difficult passage in 1 Corinthians, dealing with an unusual circumstance, Paul hints at the power of presence. As we noted in the previous chapter, a serious incidence of sexual immorality had occurred in the church: a man was living in a sexual relationship with his father's wife (his stepmother). Worse still, the church appeared to be complacent about it. Paul asked them to remedy the situation by calling a public meeting and, presumably in the absence of the offending man, handing him 'over to Satan for the destruction of the flesh, so that his spirit may be saved on the day of the Lord' (5:5, NRSV). This is hardly an easy verse to understand! Presumably it means that the man would be subject to some judgment from the church, which would lead to repentance.

Paul says that in the midst of this assembly, 'my spirit is present with the power of our Lord Jesus' (v. 4, NRSV). It would be good to be able to ask him what he meant by this, but it seems that in some way he expected his spirit to be present when the church assembled with him in mind and in their prayers. His presence, even though unseen, was acting as a kind of authorisation of the judgment on this unfortunate man. At the very least, the argument must have run as follows: if Paul's spirit (when recalled) lent power, authority and possibly comfort without his actual presence, how much more powerful must it have been when he was both physically and spiritually present among them. Our physical presence as ministers and pastors can, of itself, be powerful, in the sense of conferring authority, comfort and hope to a community.

An example springs to mind. Like many others, in April 2010 I was detained with some of my family for five extra days' stay overseas (in our case, St Petersburg). A little-known Icelandic volcano was emitting so much ash that the world's airlines were brought to a virtual standstill. When we eventually arrived home, we had missed one weekend and a few other events, but what surprised me was the relief that our return seemed to bring to our congregation. There was even spontaneous applause in the church during the Sunday morning service following our arrival. It only confirmed what I already suspected—that a good deal of pastoral work is, in a sense, about simply being there and having people know that you are there.

This is not an excuse for inertia but there is an undeniable truth that presence is significant, in a mysterious but powerful way. The effect of the pastor's presence (without wanting to exaggerate) can be to provide some kind of spiritual shelter or comfort for the whole community simply by being there.

Equally, re-entering the work of leadership after a period away, especially after a holiday, often feels to me like putting on a spiritual 'yoke' again (see Matthew 11:29). This can be hard to explain to those who have not had the experience, but it is nonetheless very real, and along with the 'yoke' it is also important to put on the spiritual armour (Ephesians 6:10–18). Often it is at the point of re-entry that some significant event takes place, or, I have sometimes noticed, it can be a time of receiving news that is profoundly challenging or disturbing. Conversely, in times of leadership vacancy, the church community can feel very vulnerable.

The strong and the weak

Another aspect of leadership for the pastor is dealing with people's spiritual sensitivities and recognising that these may vary greatly. On at least two occasions Paul taught about handling divergent views on particular issues that arose in Jewish/Gentile churches in the first century. The foundational question in these instances revolved around how to treat meat offered to idols (see 1 Corinthians 10:23–33; Romans 14). Paul knew that a Christian with a sensitive conscience found it repugnant to think of eating meat that had been previously offered to idols (see Romans 14:2). By contrast, a Christian with a more permissive conscience viewed meat offered to idols as no more than food, for which thanksgiving to God might be given before eating. The temptations for each person, whether strong or weak in faith, are explained succinctly by Paul: 'The man who eats everything must not look down on him who does not, and the man who does not eat everything must not condemn the man who does, for God has accepted him' (Romans 14:3).

The temptation of expressing superiority can face the person whose conscience permits them to do something that is of dubious value to another. At the same time, the temptation of condemning another is open to the person who prohibits something that they regard as patently wrong. Paul's advice is to act in love, which usually means that the person with a strong and permissive conscience should refrain from offending the one with the more scrupulous and sensitive conscience. He concludes, 'If your brother is distressed because of what you eat, you are no longer acting in love. Do not by your eating destroy your brother for whom Christ died' (v. 15). On the other side of the argument, although the Christian with the strong conscience should not cause the more sensitive Christian to stumble, that should not be a reason for the latter to speak ill of what is basically good. The general rule for everyone is 'Let us therefore make every effort to do what leads to peace and to mutual edification' (v. 19).

The question for the pastor today is: are these principles still applicable and, if so, to what kind of issues might they apply? Some Christians would see no problem in letting a church hall to a yoga or tai chi class, while others would find it deeply objectionable; some are more than happy with alternative therapies such as homeopathy, aromatherapy or acupuncture, while others are more than a little suspicious; some will read the Harry Potter books with relish, while others are cautious, worrying that they promote witchcraft; and so the list goes on. Some in our church were happy for a Muslim wedding reception to take place in our hall, seeing it as an opportunity for contact with a different part of our community, while others saw it in some way as compromising our witness as a church. The principle for resolving such issues has been proposed by Paul—not offending the faith of those who find such things objectionable.

In my experience, most of these issues can be dealt with quietly. For example, all new bookings of our hall are referred to me, and judicious teaching about potentially controversial subjects is provided in church services from time to time. Indeed, we have found it useful to have ongoing teaching on such subjects as war, science and faith, creationism and evolution, assisted dying, abortion, homosexuality and mental health—all of which have been seminal in airing the issues and examining positions held, in the light of scriptural teaching or principles.

Identifying gifts

A pastor will also have responsibility for encouraging people into ministry and identifying and using their gifts. Paul had a dynamic view of the church as a community of people to whom the Spirit had bestowed all manner of gifts for its own well-being as well as for its mission in the world. His favourite metaphor for the church was the body of Christ, and he used it extensively in 1 Corinthians 12—14, as well as in Romans 12:3–7. He also writes, in Ephesians, that the church is equipped by the ascended Christ with a fivefold ministry, of which pastoral care is one aspect; in Ephesians the church is seen as a dynamic community, equipped by this essential fivefold ministry for its own growth to maturity and for works of service in the world (see 4:11–13). In the context of this understanding of the church, the pastor, who is often the principal leader of the church, has the task of identifying the gifts of the people, giving training in their use, encouraging their expression and making space for their flourishing in the church and its wider mission. It is one of his most important functions, as without it the church will fail to be dynamic, becoming stunted in its growth and constricted in its mission—which will make the flock increasingly dependent and probably frustrated. All this is predicated on the need for the pastor to know her people, just as Jesus knows his own sheep or followers (John 10:14).

There is a wide range of gifts to discover in the body of Christ. Paul speaks of preaching, teaching, healing, prophecy, tongues, mercy, administration, faith, discernment, knowledge and wisdom, to name but a few. He assures us that each person in the church has 'the manifestation of the Spirit… for the common good', so no one is without some gift for service (1 Corinthians 12:7). Although the gifts are varied, they have the common aim of building up the church and extending its mission.

One way of identifying and releasing ministry in the church is through training. At each stage of my ministry, I have been committed to training church members in ministry, which has meant making sure that they have a firm grounding in their faith and are getting to grips with scripture and learning about pastoral care, public speaking, spiritual disciplines and personal development. This kind of training, whether through home-made courses run locally or regionally or through resources provided by other agencies, is essential if gifting is to be identified, trained, encouraged and released. Quite apart from all this, training sends a powerful signal to the members of the church that their gifts are valuable and need to be deployed. The importance of this pastoral task of training and deploying God's people is irrefutable, therefore, but to do this work the pastor must be able to share in the ministry without relinquishing his leadership role. He therefore needs to be able to collaborate.

Collaboration

In the last 20 years, collaboration has become a key concept in the tool-kit of ministry. In my own Anglican denomination, the need for clergy to work collaboratively has in part been forced upon them by a greatly reduced number of paid clergy trying to lead the same number of parishes. This fact has radically altered perceptions of how ministry should be conducted. One small village I look after has about 30 houses but no shops or pubs, and it stands at the top of a hill on a no through road. Until 1947 it had its own rector tending a population of no more than 100 souls—a way of life that left the priest free to pursue such hobbies as botany, bee-keeping and antiquarian research. Such a 'cure of souls' has long since ended, but the understanding that an individual clergyman was able to undertake all the pastoral care, teaching and leading of services with little or no collaboration from others was commonplace. Today, the reduction in paid clergy, together with a deeper understanding that all the baptised laity have a role to play in the church's worship, mission and ministry, has highlighted the need for effective collaborative ministry. The role of the minister is to activate the laity rather than simply being supported by the laity in the conduct of her duties.

Paul made it clear that he never worked alone; he appears to have always had companions. He was brought by Barnabas to Antioch, where they led the church together (Acts 11:26). When he set out on his first missionary journey (13:1–3), he went with Barnabas and John Mark. Mark, as we know, returned to Jerusalem before the end of the mission and was subsequently barred by Paul from accompanying him on his next journey. This caused a split with Barnabas, who still wanted to take John Mark along (15:38–39). The perils of collaborative ministry are well illustrated here. Relationships have to be worked at, personality types appreciated, common objectives understood and many blemishes overlooked or forgiven.

Despite this setback, no doubt caused by both sides coming from differing perspectives, Paul remained committed to working with companions, who now included Timothy, Titus and Silas—people upon whom he became very dependent in the years ahead. He may have remained the leader but the ministry was shared. Whenever a congregation was settled, he appointed not one but several leaders to be in charge (see, for example, the appointment of elders to the churches founded during the first missionary journey, at Lystra, Iconium and Pisidian Antioch: 14:23). Likewise, having stayed in Ephesus for at least two years, Paul appointed elders or leaders there, whom he later called to Miletus so that he could exhort them before his return to Jerusalem and arrest (see the moving account in Acts 20:17–38). Such collaborative leadership of the local church is a pattern to follow.

There is a well-known African proverb that says, 'If you want to walk fast, walk alone; if you want to walk far, walk together.' These words contain a lot of wisdom. Churches can suffer from the overactive visionary who becomes distanced from his congregation because they cannot own his enthusiasms. Not only that, but unless a team can lead forward the vision for the church, it is impossible for that vision to become truly embedded in the community. To walk far, we must walk together towards shared objectives and commonly agreed goals. How we arrive at these goals in order to share in these objectives is what we will consider in the final part of this chapter.

Vision by listening

To summarise what we have considered so far, a pastor is called to be (among other things) a reconciler and a reconciling influence in the community that he or she leads; to lead in the interests of those with a 'weak' conscience while not allowing them to speak ill of something that is not evil in itself and is actually permissible for those with a 'strong' conscience; to be a presence that mediates the peace of God; to identify the gifts of the baptised people of God and to collaborate in leadership with them. All this is a tall order for anyone, but the challenge does not quite end there. In most churches, the pastor is probably also the principal leader, and he may often be ill-equipped through training, or maybe through temperament, to give that leadership. He will lead with elders or deacons or a church council and sometimes with a staff team. Sometimes this kind of leadership role can sit uncomfortably with those innate pastoral gifts that would rather nurture than lead, rather foster than challenge, and rather comfort than confront attitudes or practices that need to change.

It is difficult to draw lessons about Paul's pastoral leadership directly from the record of his ministry in the Acts of the Apostles, because most of that record chronicles his missionary work as an evangelist and apostle rather than as a pastor. We know that on at least three occasions he spent reasonable lengths of time in different places—in Antioch (11:25–26), Corinth (18:11) and Ephesus (19:10)—which must have opened up the potential for a more pastoral ministry. Having said that, in Antioch and Corinth he chiefly taught, while in Ephesus he was engaged principally in evangelism. For the most part, Paul was an itinerant evangelist to the Jews and the Gentiles and then a church planter in Asia and Europe, with a longing to go to Rome that was fulfilled through his arrest in Jerusalem, subsequent trials and appeal to Caesar (25:11b). However, we can also see, from the way he went about his missionary journeys, the principles on which he based his ministry.

Paul's main aim was to make known the gospel and bring about obedience to God through active faith (Romans 1:5, 16), but, having planted that seed of true faith, he worked tirelessly through both teaching and pastoral care for the maturity of his flock (Colossians 1:28; Ephesians 4:13). Paul was also guided by a vision of what he wanted to achieve, which is perhaps best set out in his epistle to the Ephesians. This letter is distinct from the others (except for Romans) as being probably sent to all the churches in the region—maybe the same seven churches and others nearby to whom John wrote from Patmos (Revelation 1:4a). Here in Ephesians we see a grand vision for the church: its existence and good functioning means that 'the wisdom of God in its rich variety might now be made known to the rulers and authorities in the heavenly places' (Ephesians 3:10). This wisdom, which is the making known of a mystery previously hidden, is that the church of Jew and Gentile is united together as one new humanity (2:15) that manifests the wisdom of God. The grace of God brings it about (3:7–8); the gifts of God in ministry make this unity both possible and effective (4:11–13); and the love of God, both understood and lived, makes for a distinctive, attractive and holy fellowship (3:18; 5:1).

Here was an overarching aim for the local church, which the gifts of evangelism and apostleship initiated but the gifts of teaching and pastoral care matured. It was equally Paul's vocation, through pastoral care, to achieve this aim, and he was supported in this work by his great vision of what the local church should be.

A few years ago, in the church that I try to lead, we undertook a process of re-envisioning. By then I had been in the parish for ten years and showed every sign of staying longer, and, unless we undertook the task, I could see that the church might become dull, frustrated and lacking any clear direction for the future. We put in place a way of taking the process forward, which became known as the listening process. At its heart was the determination to listen to what God might have to say to the church at this stage of its life. With the blessing of the church council, a steering group of about eight was set up to oversee the process, made up of people both skilled in prayerfully listening to God and representative of different parts of the church's ministry and age groups within it. Apart from one meeting to answer questions, I took no part in the steering group myself, although many thought that I should, because I felt that the church would more readily accept its findings as God's leading if they knew there was no overt or covert influence by the leader. It was this leadership through trust and confidence that the Spirit would guide the church that, in the end, proved so powerful.

For the best part of a year, the whole church set out to listen to God, whether in small prayer gatherings called triplets, in larger prayer gatherings or on prayer walks around the parish. On one memorable occasion, our curate, Mike, replaced the evening service with a walk around the neighbourhood, asking us to observe its sights, sounds and atmosphere prayerfully, and then record anything we sensed that God may have been saying through our awareness.

At the end of the year's listening, a record of people's insights was produced, capturing what we believed God might be saying. A process of discernment began, at the end of which the insights were grouped under three headings: growing in prayer, going out to our community and becoming aware of our individual vocations. The final stage of the process was named 'Answering the call' and revolved around allowing these three commitments to shape our ministry as a church. The process had drawn the church together.

Two years later we are still engaged in responding to each of those calls. We have been writing and using a vocations course for church members, finding ways for the church to pray more effectively together, beginning a new youth work among the groups of marginalised young people in our community who are often on the edge of criminal behaviour and exclusion from school, and, lastly, engaging in a new form of mission (called 'More to life') by meeting on the common ground of shared passions and interests with the wider community. None of this means that we have 'arrived' in any way but the experience has given the church a sense of purpose and unity in its life together. For my part, I have found it to be a way of enabling leadership. It could be described as the people of God listening to the Spirit of God under the leadership of the church.

Paul himself would probably not have been involved in a process quite like this, but the principles would have been familiar to him. He was often guided, sometimes very directly, by the Spirit (see Acts 13:2, the call to mission at Antioch in the context of the varied gifting of the leadership team; and Acts 16:7–10, the call to Macedonia). He recognised that members of the church had gifts of discernment, wisdom and knowledge. He subscribed to the notion of momentum in God's work and the Spirit's leading, and listening was the surest way of becoming dependent on the will of God through prayer.

Among all the other responsibilities of the pastor, the task of leading is perhaps most significant. It is no good having healthy, well-tended 'sheep' if they spend their lives going round in circles. Only leadership can provide the right context for church members to grow to maturity and learn to exercise leadership themselves. As we have already seen clearly, the tasks of the pastor are considerable. It is time to consider the tools that he or she must wield in the pursuit of these objectives.

Part 3

The tools of a pastor

Chapter 7
Prayer

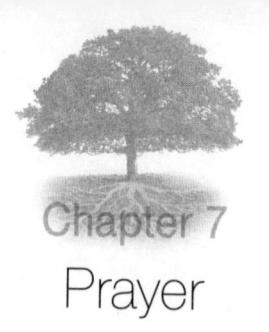

If the goals that we have set out for Paul's pastoral ministry are correct—right thinking, right living, right relationships and right leadership—how on earth could they have been achieved among all the struggles and pressures of those infant churches in the Roman empire? Paul knew that only God could accomplish such things and that prayer was the chief means whereby they might be realised. For Paul, in contrast to so many of us, there was no divorce between theology and spirituality, between teaching and praying, between prayer and action. He knew that knowledge of God had to involve dependence on him, eloquence needed to be paired with passionate conviction, and activity had to be based on God's clear leading through prayer. Otherwise, the ministry would be a sterile, man-made effort. Even if it appeared elegant, educative and informative, it would lack the power of God truly at work.

Most of Paul's epistles contain prayer for either the whole church community that he was addressing or particular individuals. All of his teaching, evangelism and apostolic work was undergirded by prayer. Even when this prayer expressed itself as worship in a Philippian gaol or remembering the churches in his personal intercessions while imprisoned in Rome, he was never more than a breath or a heartbeat away from raising others or himself in prayer to God (see Acts 16:25; Philippians 1:3–11).

All too often in ministry, prayer gets squeezed out. Some

bishops talk of the poverty of prayer among their clergy. One survey is said to have found that clergy, let alone lay members, pray for only five minutes a day. For Paul, prayer was his very existence: words such as 'always', 'all' and 'at all times' abound in his descriptions of his praying. His ministry literally began in prayer: when the understandably reluctant Ananias was told to go to the house of Judas on Straight Street and ask for a man from Tarsus named Saul, he found Paul praying (Acts 9:11). Paul remained prayerful in all parts of his ministry, whether as apostle, evangelist, prophet, teacher or pastor. More than that, his prayer was didactic, carefully attuned to the spiritual needs of those to whom he wrote. In his letters, he describes his prayers for each of the churches he cared for, and, in so doing, demonstrates how his teaching and exhortation hung together with his praying. For example, writing to the Philippians, whose life together was unblemished except for minor disagreements (see 4:2), he prays that their love might abound more and more (1:9) and teaches them to look not only to their own interests but also to the interests of others (2:4).

The origin of praying

It would be fascinating to have asked Paul what the difference was between his praying as a zealous orthodox Jew (indeed, a Pharisee) and as a Christian. No doubt it would be expressed, for the most part, in a new understanding of the fatherhood of God, as well as confidence in praying in the name of Jesus and being directed by the Spirit. In other words, the Trinity would not be far away from his thinking (see Ephesians 2:18). Of course, in some of their most heartfelt praying (notably in those prayers recorded in the Psalms), the Jews clearly understood God's tender love towards his people as well as to all who are especially vulnerable, such as the widow, orphan and stranger. Nevertheless it was Jesus who chiefly expressed new intimacy with God the Father, calling him 'Abba'. This is an everyday word in Aramaic, used by Palestinian children for their 'daddy'—someone upon whom they can gladly and confidently call at any hour of need, excitement, wonder or pain.

I am writing this the day before Fathers' Day, when many cards will be exchanged between grateful children and fathers. Sadly, though, many fathers will receive no cards because there is estrangement, bitterness, regret and unforgiveness between them and their child, something that is all too common in our society. We need healthy contact with our fathers, and what Jesus illustrated through all his prayers (except his cry of dereliction on the cross) was that we should address God as Abba, 'Daddy', as a sign of the close, intimate, confident and self-disclosing relationship that we are invited to share with him.

In two powerful pieces of teaching about prayer, Paul emphasises that the clearest mark of our position as members of the Christian family is that when we first believe (when we are adopted into God's family), the Spirit within us calls out, 'Abba, Father' from our hearts (Galatians 4:6). Likewise, in Romans 8:16, he elaborates the point a little, saying that this call of 'Abba' comes from the fact that 'the Spirit himself testifies with our spirit that we are God's children'. The same Spirit interprets our deepest soul yearnings, however inarticulate or imprecise they may be, with groans that are too deep for words (v. 26). Such groans often frame the painful question 'Why?' which we ask when loss, pain and suffering come our way and our trust in the goodness of God is put to severe test.

The sense of God's fatherhood also involved intimacy and presence for Paul. This intimate and confiding nature of God the Father is touchingly presented in William Young's novel *The Shack*, where the Father is portrayed as a muffin-making, constantly reassuring black woman called Papa. Even if this portrayal is at the cost of the power, majesty and otherness of God (and may be offensive to some), it serves to shatter any preconceptions of a distant, reserved, rule-making, head-teacher kind of father (which is too often people's idea of the fatherhood of God). Perhaps the fourth-century bishop and defender of orthodoxy Hilary of Poitiers agreed with this picture of the motherly maleness of the Father when he said that the Son of God comes from the 'womb of the Father', thus affirming that God's fatherhood includes and does not exclude his motherhood.[30]

To such a great vision of God as Father, Paul bowed the knee when praying for the Ephesians: 'kneeling before the Father' he pleaded for their greater illumination as to the extent of the love of God, which, he said, was simultaneously and paradoxically beyond knowing (2:14–19). Indeed, for Paul, 'Father' was the Christian title for God, a unique revelation brought by the Son but made real to our spirits by the Holy Spirit. The Fatherhood of God was the beginning point of his praying (as it is for all Christian prayer) but it was also the springboard of his pastoral care, as he prayed to the Father for the church to know him more deeply and reflect him more accurately.

The pathways of Paul's praying

Paul has left us a remarkable legacy of his praying, recorded in his letters to the churches. In those letters, the usual initial greetings (see, for example, 1 Corinthians 1:3) are entwined with prayerful good wishes, but he also gives us lengthy prayers for four of the seven churches to whom he wrote. His letters to the Romans, Corinthians and Galatians (the remaining three churches) record no particular prayer of any length. In the case of the Roman church, this may be because he did not found the church or because his main intention was to introduce himself and his gospel rather than writing a letter of pastoral correction to them. With the Corinthian church, he may have felt the need to keep the content of his praying private, so tempestuous was his relationship with them. And for the Galatians, his response to their errors was so passionate that perhaps he could not so much as pause to record his prayer for them before launching into his fiery response to their misguided beliefs. We shall therefore look briefly at his prayers for the congregations of the Ephesians, Philippians, Colossians and Thessalonians.

The first of these churches to be planted was at Philippi, founded in response to the dream given to Paul in Troas, asking him to come over and help the Macedonians (Acts 16:9). The church was planted in dramatic circumstances (vv. 11–40), and Paul wrote to its congregation from his prison cell in Rome, towards the end of his ministry. There is an overriding pastoral theme to the letter, encouraging unity of heart and mind in their fellowship and life together. To this end, Paul wrote of the mind they had in common in Christ Jesus, who 'made himself nothing, taking the very nature of a servant, being made in human likeness' (2:7), and he prayed for them that 'your love may abound more and more in knowledge and depth of insight' (1:9). In other words, his prayer followed their reported needs and his own discernment of what was needful for their fellowship. Discerning love was required so that unity would result from appreciating and developing this common mind in Christ, bringing agreement to some who were out of sorts with each other, and enabling their mission to the world (2:15).

Not far away was Thessalonica, where Paul went after his eventful visit to Philippi. It was an important centre of population then, as now, commanding the routes into central Greece as well as being a major seaport in the Eastern Mediterranean region. Paul stayed there only three weeks to found the church, so great was the animosity of the local Jews towards him, but the Thessalonian Christians appeared to have grasped the faith quickly and, in particular, the hope of the return of Christ. Their life together prompted Paul to continual thanksgiving, because of '[their] work produced by faith, [their] labour prompted by love, and [their] endurance inspired by hope' (1 Thessalonians 1:2–4).

If the focus of Paul's prayer for the Philippians was that they would develop a maturing love (see Philippians 1:9–11), and if, for the Thessalonians, his prayer was essentially a note of thanksgiving, for the Ephesians he prayed for both empowering knowledge and love. Ephesus was a place known for its practice of magic or occult arts, so the Ephesians, and any other neighbouring churches to which the epistle was directed, needed to have revealed to them the authority and power of Christ. Thus Paul prayed 'that you may know the hope to which he has called you... and his incomparably great power for us who believe' (Ephesians 1:18–19). This was their need, so this was what Paul prayed for, along with the power to 'grasp how wide and long and high and deep is the love of Christ' (3:18). For Paul, knowing Christ was only possible through revelation, which enabled Christians to grasp in part what is otherwise unknowable (1:17–19). True knowledge, stemming from enlightenment through the

Spirit of wisdom and revelation, was what Paul prayed for, so that they would grasp the full extent of God's power for them in Christ.

Not far from Ephesus was the church at Colossae. Like the church at Rome, it had not been planted by Paul but rather through the preaching of Epaphras (see Colossians 1:7; 4:12). The Christians there were susceptible to a heresy doing the rounds in the area, which promised greater 'fullness' to those who added to their faith the belief in a Gnostic form of Judaism. This belief emphasised the need for angelic powers and various practices that had the appearance of holiness but were actually superfluous to inheriting salvation (see 2:23). Paul argued that all we need is in Christ and that any addition to him is, in fact, a subtraction from him. Accordingly he prayed for the Colossians that they would have 'knowledge of his will through all spiritual wisdom and understanding' and, consequently, would 'live a life worthy of the Lord' (1:9–10). Once again, Paul's praying followed his diagnosis of their needs, which informed the basis of his intercession for them.

Paul the mystic?

For Paul, prayer was not only a means of bringing maturity to the churches, but also a means of entering (incidentally rather than deliberately) an almost mystical experience of God and the heavenly world he inhabits. Some would baulk at the idea of Paul being described as a mystic when it comes to prayer, yet there are aspects to his praying that place him as a somewhat unlikely father of the mystic tradition. The aspects of prayer that he shares with this tradition are:

- the act of turning everything that happened to him into a way of knowing Jesus more intimately and profoundly (Philippians 3:10).
- experiences in prayer that are best described as either ecstatic or revelatory in the extreme (2 Corinthians 12:2).
- an acute sense, at times, of battling with the 'spiritual forces of evil in the heavenly realms' (Ephesians 6:12b).

Paul frequently describes the Christian as a person who is 'in Christ'. To be in Christ was the outcome of faith, of being reconciled to God and receiving the Spirit (2 Corinthians 5:17). As so often in his teaching, there are two aspects to this understanding of being 'in Christ': firstly, a new way of seeing ourselves, and secondly, a realisation of what it means from day to day. Frequently he enjoins on his readers to become what they have already been made. Prayer is the means of realising our fellowship with Christ more intimately and profoundly so that it becomes the way of turning all human experience into an opportunity to 'know' him more deeply. Nowhere is this more vividly expressed than when he writes to the Philippians from gaol in Rome, setting out his ambition 'to know Christ and the power of his resurrection and the fellowship of sharing in his sufferings, becoming like him in his death' (3:10)—presumably by his own experience of persecution and suffering through Christ. Such an ambition allows Paul to take all experience, whether suffering or elation, and use it as a way of entering more deeply through prayer into fellowship with Christ.

Although Paul is not underwriting belief in the stigmata (receiving the signs of Christ's wounds on the cross in your own body), it is possible to see where such a train of thought comes from ('becoming like him in his death': v. 10b). Teresa of Avila described prayer as 'nothing but an intimate sharing between friends, being often alone with him who we know loves us'. She regarded all the events of life, both good and bad, as grist to the mill of her relationship with Christ. The lesson is surely that all experiences of suffering or joy may be used as a means of knowing Christ more deeply and enjoying his friendship.

The ecstatic aspect of Paul's prayer was one that he shared reluctantly with the Corinthians to substantiate his claim of being a true apostle, in no way inferior to the 'superlative apostles' (2 Corinthians 11:5, RSV) who mesmerised them. The main temptation in mysticism is that of seeking experience rather than God himself. The reason for seeking God in prayer is to worship him and plead for his kingdom to come; if some mystical experience comes as a byproduct, it is a sign of his grace, not of the success of our prayer. For Paul, his credentials as an apostle were his teaching, his sufferings (2 Corinthians 11:23–33), the signs performed by him (Romans 15:19) and the revelations given to him. So he described modestly a man in Christ (himself) 'who fourteen years ago was caught up to the third heaven. Whether it was in the body or out of the body I do not know—God knows' (2 Corinthians 12:2). If this spiritual experience was not mystical, then what is? Such experiences gave him a revelation, an exaltation of spirit and a certainty of a realm where Christ ruled, beyond the mortal world, and this gave added urgency, confidence and exuberance to his message. But lest he became too confident, he was also, as we shall see, given a 'thorn in the flesh' (v. 7).

Finally, Paul realised that to pray was to engage in a mysterious spiritual battle. The battle is mysterious because it is hard to quantify the effect of praying in the ongoing warfare in 'heavenly places', glimpsed in the book of Revelation and mentioned by Paul especially in his epistle to the Ephesians. But the belief that prayer made a difference to spiritual outcomes on earth was never in doubt for Paul. Famously, in writing to the Ephesians he portrayed the Christian as a Roman soldier, but clad in spiritual armour, stating that 'our struggle is not against flesh and blood, but against the rulers, against the authorities, against the powers of this dark world and against the spiritual forces of evil in the heavenly realms' (6:12). Because of the nature of this struggle, the Christian was to put on 'the full armour of God' (v. 13). This struggle with the devil was a major part of the experience of the desert hermits who occupied the fastnesses of Syria, Egypt and Palestine from the fourth century onwards. Thus Hyperichius, a desert monk, said, 'Temptations come to us in all kinds of ways. We ought to put on full armour, and then we shall seem to them to be expert soldiers when they attack us'.[31]

Paul's mystical praying was a necessary basis for his pastoral care of the churches, his apostolic evangelism and his prophetic insight. He was utterly committed to prayer because he was completely convinced that prayer 'was the slender nerve that moved the hand of God'.[32] He was in no doubt that prayer changed things. It was the means of transforming anxiety into peace—a peace that passed all understanding (Philippians 4:6). It was through prayer that opportunities for preaching the gospel came (Colossians 4:3–4; 2 Thessalonians 3:1). It was through prayer that he was repeatedly delivered, not avoiding suffering but being enabled to endure it, to continue to bear witness through it and to know God's love and faithfulness (2 Corinthians 1:9–11).

Ultimately his praying was the expression of his gratitude to and dependence upon God who had chosen him to be the apostle to the Gentiles. Prayer was also the channel whereby his weaknesses became his strengths—the means of recycling all his experiences, both negative and positive, in the cause of deeper fellowship with Jesus. To this profound insight about ministry in general and about Paul's ministry in particular, we must now turn.

Chapter 8

Strength and weakness

Who knew weakness as Paul did? Frequently he would allude to his weaknesses, recounting the sufferings that underlay them (see 2 Corinthians 6:3–10). Paul had a profound understanding of the relationship between God's grace and our weakness. He realised that human weakness, when offered in faith, was never a bar to God's power being at work; in fact, paradoxically, it probably enhanced God's ability to work, for no human pride interfered. There are two passages in his epistles that especially demonstrate the power of weakness in God's hands: the 'hymn to Christ' in Philippians 2:6–11 and his own extraordinary personal testimony of God's power working in his weakness, in 2 Corinthians 12:9.

In the Philippian hymn, Jesus, although the pre-existent Word, 'did not consider equality with God something to be grasped' but rather emptied himself and 'made himself nothing, taking the very nature of a servant' (vv. 6–7). In other words, he made himself weak, vulnerable and dependent on others, whether his parents or friends. In a further description of this 'emptying', Paul tells the Corinthians that we 'know the grace of our Lord Jesus Christ, that though he was rich, yet for your sakes he became poor, so that you through his poverty might become rich' (2 Corinthians 8:9). Jesus assumed vulnerability, weakness and simplicity of life, having minimal possessions and no home. He described himself as having nowhere to lay his head (Luke 9:58b) and lost even the clothes on his back before his death (23:34b).

For most people, strength comes from wealth, education and high social status, but Jesus possessed none of those things. Rather, having possessed everything, he assumed nothing; having been exalted, he humbled himself. This was the example that inspired Paul and, in the end, made him the exemplar of the saying that 'when I am weak, then I am strong' (2 Corinthians 12:10b).

Paul lived in a world that depended on strength. The Roman world was a harsh and cruel one where power was conferred by force of arms. The Roman military machine was fearsome. It took the martial skills developed in Greece (particularly in Sparta, Athens and Macedon, which had first stopped and then overthrew the Persian empire) and turned them into a systematic fighting force, unequalled in the Western world. Rebellion, wherever it occurred, was crushed by disciplined troops, and the will of the empire was enforced by crucifixion and slavery. Into such an empire, which had occupied Israel, came a defenceless Galilean preacher, Jesus of Nazareth, who declared, 'Blessed are the meek, for they will inherit the earth' (Matthew 5:5) and said to a Roman provincial governor, in a supreme moment of vulnerability, 'My kingdom is not of this world' (John 18:36).

Paul saw in the story of Jesus of Nazareth how supreme political and military strength was challenged by complete vulnerability and seeming weakness, but was nonetheless invested with another kind of power—a power made perfect in weakness. Paul understood that through the resurrection a brand new world or kingdom had come into existence, which would grow and endure for ever, outlasting all others, and at its centre was this principle of seeming weakness overcoming more obvious strength. In fact, this was the fulfilment of the vision in Daniel 7, in which successive empires are overthrown until Daniel sees 'one like a son of man coming with the clouds of heaven'(v. 13) and establishing an eternal kingdom. The human figure is described as entering the presence of the Ancient of Days, to be given 'authority, glory and sovereign power' (v. 14).

Having identified Jesus as this Son of Man, Paul knew that, in the end, his seeming weakness was both the root of and the route to all authority, power and strength. It was the root of all authority because it increased dependence on God, who was the final source of all authority (see John 19:11), and it was the route to authority because such dependence enhances and curiously exhibits an authority that is greater than any show of human power. Paul was to make this clear as a pastor-teacher to his churches, and never more so than in his relationship with the Corinthians.

Paul and the Corinthians

Paul's relationship with the Corinthians appears to have been tempestuous at best, tortured at worst. His correspondence with them (of which we have two long letters out of, possibly, an original four) pulsates with a passion that is discernible across the millennia. Misunderstandings crept into their relationship because the Corinthians, who were a socially mixed church, found that Paul did not fit with many of their cherished values, several of which arose from their racy Greco-Roman seaport culture. They valued style, form and outward show, whereas Paul was comparatively unpolished in his way of speaking. They liked their leaders to look good but Paul's appearance was not especially impressive. They admired rhetoric and the skills of oratory but Paul's preaching was 'not with wise and persuasive words' (1 Corinthians 2:4). He did not demand expenses from them—which, curiously, might have impressed them; rather, he worked so as not to burden them (1 Corinthians 9:15–18; 2 Corinthians 11:7) His was not a flamboyant ministry compared with what he calls sarcastically 'those superlative apostles' (2 Corinthians 11:5, RSV). Although he validated the Corinthians' more sensational and supernatural gifts, he said that they were valueless unless accompanied and fulfilled by love (1 Corinthians 13:1–3).

All this grated with the Corinthians—so impressionable, easily flattered and susceptible to occasional sexual misdemeanours of a flagrant kind (1 Corinthians 5:1); given over sometimes to excess in their *agape* feasts, so that the poor were excluded (11:20–22); willing to hire lawyers to settle differences (6:1–6) and easily driven into competing factions (3:3–5). Fundamentally, they admired strength in the true Roman way—oratory, physical presence, sophistication and demanding leadership—but Paul's strength was of a different kind, which they had to get used to. It was a strength that came from weakness.

The weakness that Paul spoke about resided in a number of things. It was present in his many sufferings, which were chronicled on several occasions, especially in his correspondence with the Corinthians (see also his account of coming to the Galatians in physical weakness, in 4:13–14). Much of this correspondence is tinged with irony, sarcasm and implied reproof. Early in his first letter to the Corinthians, Paul writes, 'Already you have all you want! Already you have become rich! You have become kings—and that without us! [Here is rich irony] How I wish that you really had become kings so that we might be kings with you!' (4:8). Then, feeling the weakness and pressure of his own life, he says, 'For it seems to me that God has put us apostles on display at the end of the procession, like men condemned to die in the arena. We have been made a spectacle to the whole universe, to angels as well as to men. We are fools for Christ, but you are so wise in Christ! We are weak, but you are strong' (vv 9–10).

In his second letter, the theme of weakness as strength becomes even more marked. He reminds the Corinthians in a memorable metaphor that 'we have this treasure [the gospel] in jars of clay to show that this all-surpassing power is from God' (4:7). Again Paul lists his sufferings, as well as their limitation in terms of their effect on him: 'hard pressed on every side, but not crushed; perplexed, but not in despair; persecuted, but not abandoned; struck down, but not destroyed' (vv. 8–9). Later in the same epistle, he recounts a long list of his deprivations on account of his apostolic ministry: 'Five times I received from the Jews the forty lashes minus one. Three times I was beaten with rods, once I was stoned, three times I was shipwrecked, I spent a night and a day in the open sea, I have been constantly on the move... and in danger' (11:24–26). In the end he concludes passionately, 'Who is weak, and I do not feel weak? Who is led into sin, and I do not inwardly burn? If I must boast, I will boast of the things that show my weakness' (vv. 29–30). And he will boast of his weakness because, as he says later, 'when I am weak, then I am strong' (12:10b).

As if the sufferings themselves were not enough to keep Paul feeling weak, he also had to contend with a 'thorn in the flesh'. He describes this affliction in the midst of an impassioned argument with the Corinthians about his credentials as an apostle. Already he has told them of the revelations he was given, which took him to either paradise or the 'third heaven' (12:2, 4), but then he explains how, to keep him from becoming either arrogant or too elated, he was given the 'thorn in the flesh'. This is likely to have been a physical disability or disease and, although he sought God for healing or its removal three times, no such relief was provided. Instead, the prophetic word came, 'My grace is sufficient for you, for my power is made perfect in weakness' (v. 9).

This was a seminal word for Paul, with deep repercussions not only for him but for all those who find themselves ministering out of a sense of weakness. There was no total healing for him, no glorious testimony of God's intervention, but rather a different testimony: the all-sufficiency of Christ in the face of protracted difficulty. This is not a denial of God's ability to heal where he chooses but it is an affirmation that God deals with each of us singly and personally, and that, come what may, his grace is sufficient, even if we would rather be released from whatever burdens we carry. The other half of the 'word' that Paul was given is a paradox, a seeming contradiction—that God's 'power is made perfect in weakness'. Could it be, then, that our strength can be a limitation to God's power at work within us? Presumably, yes! It is this weakness that at times gives rise to 'groaning' (see Romans 8:22–27; 2 Corinthians 5:4) but also creates the conditions of dependence in which God's power in us may be perfected.

You don't have to read far into the lives of God's people to see that weakness is often an accompaniment of their calling. There was Moses, loath to take up his call because he could not speak eloquently (Exodus 4:10). There was Jeremiah, frightened of the faces of those to whom he was sent (Jeremiah 1:6–9, KJV). There was Augustine of Hippo, preferring the quiet seclusion of a monastery to the demanding life of a bishop, who had to be literally dragged from that seclusion, or the monk Anselm, who likewise was reluctantly pressed into service as the Archbishop of Canterbury. We could think of Martin Luther, taking on a corrupt papacy that was determined to silence him, and facing times of severe spiritual struggle; or the 18th-century poet William Cowper, a friend of John Newton, who struggled with depression and asked, 'Where is the peace that once I knew?' There was Christina Rossetti, the hymn writer who gave us one of the loveliest Christmas carols, 'In the bleak midwinter', but struggled with grave feelings of guilt and inadequacy. David Watson, the parish priest and evangelist, often up half the night with bouts of asthma and frequently feeling depressed, was taken by cancer in his early 50s, by which time, under God, he had changed the lives of thousands. More recently, there is another minister, Mike Wenham, struggling with Motor Neurone Disease, who tells his story bravely, humorously and poignantly in his book *My Donkey Body*.[33] His remarkable account gives hope to others and bears witness to the gift of life in a world increasingly bent on assisted suicide as a way out of ongoing suffering.

These are a few people who have known weakness firsthand but have testified to the mysterious way in which God's presence has powerfully shone through their physical or emotional frailty. Many others can say that when they were spent, tired, ill or just weak, God came and used them in ways that he did not when they were healthy, sleek, well groomed and confident in themselves. Why? For 'when I am weak, then I am strong'!

Frankly, I can't imagine Paul in a white suit bestriding a dais, microphone in hand, heralding another miracle live on satellite TV—but I can see him in the favelas of Brazil, the cinder apartment blocks of China or the shanty towns of Mumbai, immersed in his apostolic labours, explaining the gospel, healing the sick and pastoring the newly transformed. Tired and worn, but still cheerful and confident, he tells of one who 'though he was rich, yet for your sakes… became poor, so that you through his poverty might become rich' and demonstrating that love in deeds of liberation (2 Corinthians 8:9). Meanwhile, he continually looks for those to whom he might speak and others whom he might train in this unlikely ministry of God's power being made perfect in weakness.

What might all this mean for our own pastoral ministry? It means that when we are at our most vulnerable, weak and beset by difficulties, we may be at our best, most accessible and approachable. When we ourselves are open about our weakness, we may help others to face theirs. Often, the healer works best as a wounded one—better able to empathise, more readily able to sympathise with the weaknesses and foibles of those he cares for. Most importantly, as pastors, we can show by our example the overriding importance of being dependent on God.

Chapter 9

Word and sacraments

There can be little doubt that the chief tools of Paul's trade as a pastor, alongside his dependence on prayer and acknowledgment of his weakness, were the word of God, the Spirit of God and the sacraments. If prayer is the context in which all effective pastoral ministry takes place, word, Spirit and sacrament form the foundation from which such ministry is conducted.

The word

With his Pharisaic background, Paul was no stranger to the significance and seriousness of God's word. The scriptures (in the first instance, the Old Testament writings) were, to him, God's very words, and so he treated them with extreme reverence. The learning, discussing and debating of the scriptures would have been the basis of his training from boyhood, so applying himself to understanding them was second nature. Finding out both their meaning and their application would have been a familiar process. What was novel, after his Damascus road experience, was reinterpreting the scriptures in the light of the knowledge that Jesus was the Messiah, the one whom the law and prophets foretold, who would fulfil the whole sacrificial system of the Old Testament.

In the first place, Paul had a clear understanding of the inspiration of the scriptures by the Spirit. He speaks of this in two places in particular. First, in a passage about the revelation of wisdom by the Spirit, he talks about the disclosure of a secret wisdom within Old Testament scripture, which was not understood by the rulers of his age (1 Corinthians 2:8). This wisdom, like human wisdom, is expressed in words, but words inspired by the Spirit. As Paul puts it, 'This is what we speak, not in words taught us by human wisdom but in words taught by the Spirit, expressing spiritual truths in spiritual words' (v. 13). These words provide authoritative, divinely inspired teaching, and it was this spiritual wisdom that was given to Paul. He was led to express it in Spirit-inspired words, which became the teaching that he conveyed to the churches through his letters and finally became part of the scriptures that we read. Occasionally, however, he was aware that his teaching arose from his own thinking—for example, what he said about marriage and remarriage (see 1 Corinthians 7:25, 40) during the critical times of persecution that the Christian community faced. Consequently, although part of our scripture, such teaching would be less binding.

Second, in writing to Timothy, Paul reminds him of the role of the scriptures in his life—how, from his infancy, he learnt from the Old Testament, from his grandmother Lois and his mother Eunice, who was a believer as well as Jewish by background (Acts 16:1; 2 Timothy 1:5). The scriptures that Timothy learnt from his family had the effect of making him wise (2 Timothy 3:15). Once again we note the connection between wisdom and the scriptures (1 Corinthians 2:13): following or putting into practice the scriptures makes for wisdom.

Not only that, but Paul goes on to say that they have the effect of 'teaching, rebuking, correcting and training in righteousness, so that the man of God may be thoroughly equipped for every good work' (2 Timothy 3:16–17). Since the scriptures are the means for forming, training and equipping the disciple, a pastor must become familiar with them, in terms of both fashioning his or her own life and using them appropriately in forming the lives of others. Timothy is given precisely this instruction by Paul, who says that he should become like 'a workman who does not need to be ashamed and who correctly handles the word of truth' (2:15). If Timothy attends to the teaching himself, he too will reach maturity and be sure of his own salvation (1 Timothy 4:16).

Likewise, a pastor will find that God's word is the chief means by which he may fashion and form the flock he leads. He must teach it continually and use it to alter a wrong mindset or uphold a healthy one. He should try to exemplify the scriptural values of grace, love, generosity and truth, which should prevail in the fellowship of the church, in public preaching, personal example and pastoral care at every level. But none of this can happen without the Spirit.

The Spirit

At the time of writing, Pentecost has just passed. When preaching at Pentecost, I often say that it is quite impossible to live the Christian life without the aid of the Spirit. We then provide opportunity for every member of the church to receive a fresh infilling of the Spirit during the service. On one occasion, preaching about the gifts of the Spirit, I stressed three of the metaphors often used to describe the Spirit's activity: fire, wind and water. Having explained the meaning of each one, I encouraged the congregation of all ages to come forward to be anointed with oil, symbolising the Spirit, and simply to say one of those words to me—'fire', 'wind' or 'water'. Their chosen word would signify how they wanted the Spirit to work in their lives: like fire, bringing cleansing and passion; like wind, bringing momentum and energy; or like water, bringing refreshment and growth. Almost everyone came forward for prayer, and, when I looked up at the end of this time of prayer, I realised that the church was empty and it was past lunch-time. Everyone was talking about it for days.

Every pastor knows that without the Spirit she can do nothing. It is the Spirit who brings conviction, encouragement, growth and gifting. If the Spirit is at work, he will point out to the consciences of people what is wrong or needful. One colleague of mine in a previous church where I served was renowned for his pastoral ministry. He did not have to labour an issue with somebody: a conversation under the gaze of his coaxing, searching eyes, which seemed to reveal people's thoughts and secrets, was enough to cause many of them to go away and deal with what they knew to be wrong or in need of serious attention. Undoubtedly it was the Spirit who worked through this pastor to bring people to such knowledge. The Spirit is, after all, the Spirit of truth (John 14:17), which does not mean doctrinal truth alone but the kind of probing truth that has to do with integrity and consistency.

The Spirit is the person of the Trinity who brings growth, maturity and wholeness in three distinct areas. Firstly, it is he who brings assurance that we belong to God, that we are his children. Paul makes this clear when he says of the believer, 'You did not receive a spirit that makes you a slave again to fear, but you received the Spirit of sonship. And by him we cry "Abba, Father". The Spirit himself testifies with our spirit that we are God's children. Now if we are children, then we are heirs—heirs of God and co-heirs with Christ' (Romans 8:15–17). It is the Spirit who, when given to the believer, cries out to God, 'Abba, Father'. It is this deep cry from the pit of our being that gives us the assurance that we are truly God's children. No amount of human endeavour can convince a person that this is truly the case, but the Spirit can do it in places that no one else can reach. The Spirit does this by working through both word and sacrament. If God's word is filled with promises that we may hold on to, it finds its symbolic power in the sacraments.

In baptism, the believer is assured of belonging to the family of God, and in the Lord's Supper she is assured of forgiveness and acceptance. In the lovely words of Cranmer's post-Communion prayer in the 1662 Prayer Book, he says that through these gifts of bread and wine received in faith, God 'assures us thereby of his goodness and favour towards us'. This happens inwardly by the Spirit. Such deep assurance of belonging to God, manifested to the believer's heart in the knowledge of receiving 'sonship', is not something that any pastor can engineer but it is something that may be relied on.

Secondly, the Spirit is the one who brings fruitfulness in the life of the people of God. Nowhere is this made clearer than in Paul's teaching on the fruit of the Spirit in Galatians 5:22–26, where he describes the Spirit's work in forming the likeness of Christ through the list of fruit that the Spirit engenders. The pastor is like a surgeon or doctor who, having pointed out the things that prevent healing and worked for their removal, then relies on the natural capacity of the body to heal itself. Likewise, Paul, having pointed out the things that prevent growth (in verses 19–21), then relies on the free reign of the Spirit in a person or community to start producing the fruit of the Spirit over a lifetime, sometimes working on a particular fruit at a particular time because of the circumstances surrounding an individual.

Thirdly, the Spirit brings to birth the gifts needed for pastoral ministry. In 1 Corinthians, Paul lists a whole sequence of gifts available to the body of Christ that are especially needful in pastoral care, including wisdom, knowledge, discernment and faith (12:7–11). The Spirit helps to fan into flame such gifts, which may otherwise lie dormant. Timothy, for instance, perhaps by virtue of his innate timidity, was not using the gifts implanted in him when Paul himself had laid hands on him and commissioned him as a church leader. Paul therefore urges him to forgo his timidity, 'for God did not give us a spirit of timidity, but a spirit of power, of love and of self-discipline' (2 Timothy 1:7), and consequently to 'fan into flame the gift of God which is in you through the laying on of my hands' (v. 6).

Likewise, a pastor requires such gifts of grace and must find ways of allowing the Spirit to fan them into flames. This may be done by belonging to a small accountability group made up of friends or contacts from college or ministerial training days, going on retreat or using a spiritual director or meeting up with local colleagues. What is important is that an atmosphere is created of honesty, vulnerability and prayer. I have learnt to value most of these ways of keeping myself on track and enabling the Spirit to stir up gifts in me.

In these ways the Spirit works in pastoral care, bringing assurance or confidence, growing fruit in our and others' lives and also providing the gifts upon which so much pastoral care depends. Thus the pastor must depend on word and Spirit to fulfil her task—and, finally, on the sacraments as well.

The sacraments

Paul must have remembered his own baptism vividly. Sitting in the house in Straight Street, blinded by his encounter with Jesus on the way to Damascus, he waited for a man named Ananias to come and lay hands on him, to receive back his sight and be filled by the Holy Spirit (Acts 9:11–17). Immediately after this visit, Paul was baptised, marking the moment when he passed from death to life, from darkness to light—the moment when, as he wrote to Titus in Crete, he was 'saved... through the washing of rebirth and renewal by the Holy Spirit' (Titus 3:5).

There is no doubt that the symbolism and grace associated with baptism would remain central to Paul's teaching about the new life that Christians enjoy. He would use baptism repeatedly as the visual symbol of both the break with an old life and the beginning of something completely new. Much of his teaching about living the Christian life would be an appeal to the event of new birth that baptism recalled and marked. Baptism is a single event with boundless consequences and meaning, and is richly described by Paul, using various metaphors such as dying to the old life (Romans 6:4), putting on a new self (Colossians 3:10) and being washed and cleansed (Titus 3:5b). It is a means of remembering what God has done for us, his people, what he has made us, to what he has called us and what still lies in the future.

The Lord's Supper would be the act of fellowship in which Jesus' death was recalled by the community of his followers until he returned. It would serve both as an act of remembering and as an act of participation in the benefits and blessings of the Lord's death. For Paul the pastor, both sacraments were integral to the journey of discipleship (see 1 Corinthians 10:1–3; Romans 6:3): baptism is the spiritual and symbolic beginning from which we may draw continual inspiration, and the Lord's Supper is the repeated place of refreshment, renewal and proclamation of our faith along the way (1 Corinthians 11:26). Together they recall what God has done in us (baptism) and for us (the Lord's Supper or Holy Communion).

The significance of baptism

Baptism is always a significant moment, whether (as I have done) baptising a pilgrim to the Holy Land in the Jordan river, baptising a new convert in the Avon river near Bath, baptising a whole family of twelve in a baptistery or taking infant or adult baptism in a church service. For each person or family, there is no doubting the power of the occasion. Throughout his letters, Paul often referred to baptism as the event that symbolised the bestowal of new life in the Spirit as well as the responsibilities of obligation on a new believer. His teaching about baptism included five different aspects, which we will consider now.

The washing away of sin

The most obvious meaning of baptism, suggested by the element of water, is washing or its spiritual equivalent, forgiveness. As already mentioned, Paul refers to baptism indirectly as 'the washing of rebirth and renewal by the Holy Spirit, whom he poured out on us generously through Jesus Christ' (Titus 3:5–6). Baptism is the outward symbol of inner cleansing—our souls being made clean. In some of the earliest teaching given to baptism candidates, by Cyril of Jerusalem in c.348, he describes baptism as an objective reminder to the candidates that all their guilt is cleansed by the grace of God. Nothing can ever again be levelled against their conscience.

Martin Luther used to recall that when, in times of spiritual struggle, he sensed the devil accusing him of past failure and questioning his assurance of salvation, he would shout,

'*Baptizatus sum!*' ('I am baptised'), recalling his baptism as a sure sign of forgiveness, cleansing and acceptance.

Union with Christ

If cleansing is the most obvious meaning of baptism, another is symbolised by the action of baptism rather than its element—the mystical union with the death and resurrection of Jesus. Paul elaborates this theme in Romans 6:4 when he says, 'We were therefore buried with him through baptism into death in order that, just as Christ was raised from the dead through the glory of the Father, we too may live a new life' (v. 4). Baptism, especially in the form of full immersion, speaks of being buried—going under the water—and rising again. It symbolises the death of our 'old self', which is buried with Christ. As we have seen in chapter 3, this does not mean that the Christian is impervious to temptation; rather, it is that the power of the old way of life has been broken, so that there is now no need to sin. This is surely what Paul means when he says, 'For we know that our old self was crucified with him so that the body of sin might be done away with, that we should no longer be slaves to sin' (v. 6).

Putting on new clothes

By the fourth century, baptism had become an impressive and profoundly moving event. The informal early church setting of a river, lake or sea had given way to ceremonies in places where the architecture was designed around the whole theology of baptism. The description of baptism in Jerusalem at the time of Cyril demonstrates this:

> After assembling in the vestibule of the baptistery the candidates, facing west and with hands stretched out,

made a formal renunciation of the devil. Then, turning to the east, they solemnly professed faith in the Trinity and in the One Baptism of Repentance. Passing into the inner chamber they took off their clothes and were anointed with exorcised oil. They were then led by the hand one by one to the font where again making formal profession of their faith they were immersed three times in the blessed baptismal water to symbolise the Redeemer's three-day sojourn in the grave. This was followed by the post-Baptismal chrismation, and after putting on white garments, the neophytes [literally 'newly enlightened'] made their way into the church where they received their first Communion.[34]

The metaphor of changing clothes springs from Paul's teaching to the Colossians, where he tells them to put to death all that would drag them back to their former way of life and instead 'clothe yourselves' (Colossians 3:5, 12) with attitudes essential to the Christian way of life. Likewise, they should 'take off [their] old self... and put on the new self, which is being renewed in knowledge in the image of its Creator' (vv. 9–10). Baptism was the time to symbolise that change of inner clothing when a candidate first believed.

Being sealed with the Spirit

The moment of baptism, or 'chrismation' (as Cyril called it), was the moment when the candidate formally received the Spirit. In Paul's own initiation he received the Spirit at the laying on of hands by Ananias, before his baptism (see Acts 9:17). From this we see that there is no strict order of initiation so much as a cluster of events, including repentance, renunciation of the devil, profession of faith, baptism and being filled with the Spirit, which ideally happen as close to each other as possible at the outset. As Michael Harper has written, 'In the early church the blessing of the Spirit's power was the normal accompaniment of conversion and not a compulsory second stage of spiritual experience. It was a gift received by faith, not a reward for progress in the Christian life.'[35]

Because of the practice of infant baptism, the reception of the Spirit became largely associated in Roman Catholic and Anglican churches with Confirmation; but Confirmation was really intended as a strengthening of the candidate by the Spirit on the occasion of adult profession of faith, rather than being the candidate's first reception of the Spirit.

Paul himself is silent on the practice of infant baptism. He may have practised household baptism, as in the case of the households of Stephanas and the Philippian gaoler (1 Corinthians 1:16; Acts 16:33), but most of his teaching about baptism related to an adult understanding of its significance. For Paul, the Spirit sealed the Christian's life, giving a down-payment here and now of something greater still to come (Ephesians 4:30). The gift of the Spirit, symbolised and offered in baptism, gives assurance of the Fatherhood of God, equips for service and also incorporates the individual believer into the body of Christ (1 Corinthians 12:13).

Being in Christ

The result of this incorporation by baptism was that the candidate was both 'in Christ' and fully incorporated into the body of Christ. Paul uses the phrase 'in Christ' 83 times in his writings.[36] Although it is sometimes used objectively, describing what God in his redemptive act has done for us in Christ (see, for example, Romans 3:24), it is also used subjectively to describe the new blessings that are in Christ for the believer (Romans 8:1). Most of all, it conveys the change of status that the Christian enjoys, in which he now shares in the new cosmic order brought about by Christ and enjoys an intimacy with him that is best described by being 'in Christ'.

The Lord's Supper

What baptism conveys to the believer at the outset of her discipleship, the Eucharist or Lord's Supper nurtures thereafter. Paul's correspondence with the Corinthian church is the only place where he explicitly teaches about the Lord's Supper. The teaching comes in the midst of a passage where Paul needs to straighten out their abuse of the sacrament, so the context is polemical, arising from their egregious use of the supper. At the outset, Paul says that their meetings in which the Lord's Supper take place 'do more harm than good' (1 Corinthians 11:17)—hardly an auspicious start to reflection on its significance! But their failures can teach us what Paul's expectations of that fellowship were. Rather than being a deep moment of unity in their fellowship, their celebration of the Lord's Supper only served to underline their divisions (v. 18); rather than using it as a means of remembering the Lord's death, they satisfied their hunger, with the more powerful or richer believers eating first (vv. 21–22). This sounds more like a Roman feast than a deeply reflective meal, calling to mind the event of Jesus' sacrificial death that inaugurated their fellowship. It should have united them in humble gratitude and service, yet some of them seem to have forgotten the fundamental purpose of the meal and were simply feasting without regard to its meaning.

As a result of these substantial blemishes on their fellowship, Paul calls the Corinthians to 'wait for each other', to eat worthily and 'examine' themselves (vv. 27, 28, 33)—none of which they were doing. The result of these failures was that God's judgment was coming upon them. Some in the congregation were weak or sick or had even 'fallen asleep': that is, they had incurred God's displeasure and been robbed of life, if not of salvation (v. 30).

Amid all the negativity, Paul still seeks to restore the meaning and mystery of the Lord's Supper, to bolster a deeply reverent view of the celebration. He appears to have received instructions from the Lord himself about it (v. 23). The words of institution (vv. 24–25) are consonant with the Gospels and are the earliest record of the Lord's words at his final meal with the disciples. Here we have Jesus taking the bread and cup, giving thanks for them both, breaking the bread and distributing the cup. The words 'This is my body' and 'This cup is the new covenant in my blood' define the significance of the bread and wine clearly without explaining the mechanics of the transformation of their substance. Twice, Paul recalls, these actions were to be repeated 'in remembrance of me'. In the years to come, the church tried to describe too precisely how they became Jesus' body and blood rather than agreeing that eating and drinking in faith were what made the symbols truly significant.

Paul goes one step further in describing the meaning of the Lord's Supper while warning the Corinthians against participating in pagan sacrifices and idol feasts, such as regularly took place at temples (see 1 Corinthians 10:14–22). The principle appears to have been that to take part in the sacrificial meal was to share in the significance of the worship at that temple; if it was a pagan shrine, then taking part in the meal was to collude with or give credence to the pagan deity being honoured. Likewise, Paul argues that sharing in the Lord's Supper was more than just eating in remembrance; it was 'a participation in the blood of Christ' and 'in the body of Christ' (v. 16). Here was a note of mystery, for we cannot adequately explain what this sharing of the Lord's body and blood amounts to, except to say that it is a spiritual feeding, nourishment and sustenance of the believer. It is more than merely remembering, more than simple recollection or recalling; the recipient is being spiritually fed in the deepest possible way in the deepest possible place.

The significance of the sacrament

Paul the pastor knew well the significance of the sacraments. Although he did not himself baptise many (1 Corinthians 1:14–16), perhaps allowing his associates or newly appointed church leaders to undertake baptisms more frequently, the significance of baptism was never far from his teaching about what God has done for his people and the nature of the calling that Christ has given to his followers. It was an ever-present reality for him. The sacraments provide essential encouragement and nurture of the pilgrim church and regular proclamation of the story of the faith in the context of community. Baptism promises the reality of new life and the Lord's Supper sustains it by providing the most intimate moment in the life of the fellowship—recalling the cost of our freedom in Christ, the price of our forgiveness and the renewal of fellowship between one another and the Lord. It is an occasion when the whole church, in heaven and earth, recalls and proclaims the Lord's death until he comes again.

Chapter 10

The pastor's heart

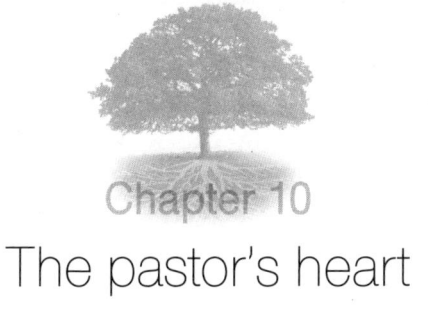

To be a true pastor is to have your heart at the very least sensitised, sometimes bruised, and just occasionally broken, either by the struggles in life of the people you care and pray for or by your care of them. Not only that, but your own pastoral ministry may be questioned, misunderstood or simply expected in a different shape or form by the very people you seek to pastor. It can be painful as well as deeply satisfying.

In the Old Testament, the high priest went before God wearing an ephod into which were sewn two onyx stones. On each of these stones were engraved the names of six of the sons of Jacob or Israel (see Exodus 28:9–12). This meant that, every time the high priest appeared before God, he carried on his shoulders the names of the tribes of Israel. I suspect that he carried them not only on his shoulders but also, in a profound way, in his heart.

Likewise, the pastor carries the hopes and yearnings of her people in her heart. As Paul himself says, as members of the body of Christ we are to 'rejoice with those who rejoice; mourn with those who mourn' (Romans 12:15). If such empathy is the calling of every member of the body of Christ, how much more is it the calling of a pastor? It also means that a true pastor can never hide his heart away to protect it from hurt or discouragement; he must be prepared to have his heart elated and dashed in almost equal measure. Any reading of Paul's writings shows the full range of emotion that he experienced in the course of caring for the many churches he either founded or sought to bring to maturity. We shall look at five ways in which his heart was extended in the challenge of pastoring these churches, which he displays in the course of his epistles.

The yearning heart of a pastor

Yearning is a common human emotion—a form of painful desiring, born of love and held in hope. There are so many human situations in which yearning plays a part. I think of a family with a father or husband serving abroad in the military, and how every day they pray and yearn for his safety amid news of mounting casualties. They yearn for his safe return. There is the yearning of a lover for news of a beloved by text or phone, and the reassurance that their love is reciprocated, or there is the yearning of a parent for news of a child now grown up and travelling the world on his or her gap year. Wherever there is love, there will be yearning.

Not surprisingly, therefore, God's love in the Old Testament is shown to be in an almost constant state of yearning for a recalcitrant Israel, who either spurned his attention or turned from his ways. The prophets, especially in the pre-exilic period when impending doom might have been averted, constantly expressed the yearning of God for reconciliation with his rebellious offspring. Few put it more tenderly than Hosea, who said:

> How can I give you up, Ephraim?
> How can I hand you over, Israel?
> How can I treat you like Admah?
> How can I make you like Zeboiim?
> My heart is changed within me;

all my compassion is aroused.
I will not carry out my fierce anger,
nor will I turn and devastate Ephraim.
For I am God and not man—
the Holy One among you.
I will not come in wrath. (Hosea 11: 8–9)

In the New Testament, too, Jesus displays deepest yearning for Jerusalem, weeping over her hardness of heart: 'O Jerusalem, Jerusalem, you who kill the prophets and stone those sent to you, how often I have longed to gather your children together, as a hen gathers her chicks under her wings, but you were not willing!' (Luke 13:34). Jesus yearned that Jerusalem would receive her meek and gentle king and would not come into judgment; but, distressingly, he knew that she would reject him.

What the prophets felt for Israel in the Old Testament and Jesus for his people, and particularly Jerusalem, in the New Testament, so a pastor will feel for his flock—the flock of God over which the Spirit has made him 'overseer' or 'shepherd' (see 1 Peter 5:2–4). There will be a yearning for the flock and individual members of it, for their spiritual and physical well-being. Undoubtedly Paul felt such yearning for several of the churches he cared for, not least for the Galatian Christians. He was perplexed that they were turning away from the gospel that he had preached to them and turning back to subservience to the law. He cried out:

> You foolish Galatians! Who has bewitched you? Before your very eyes Jesus Christ was clearly portrayed as crucified… After beginning with the Spirit, are you now trying to attain your goal by human effort? Have you suffered so much

for nothing—if it really was for nothing? Does God give
you his Spirit and work miracles among you because you
observe the law, or because you believe what you heard?'
(3:1, 3–5)

Paul's perplexity was intense. He also yearned for them, saying, 'My dear children, for whom I am again in the pains of childbirth until Christ is formed in you…' (4:19). His yearning was like that of a woman in labour, bringing Christ to birth in them through pain and struggle.

Today, a pastor will yearn for many different things for her flock. It may be a yearning for the church to eschew some false theology or teaching or to grasp an aspect of the gospel that has hitherto been evaded or misunderstood. Or the yearning may be more personal—for instance, for families who have fallen out over a relatively trivial matter to find reconciliation. The pastor may yearn for healing where disease has struck the same family again, or he may yearn for a couple to have a child, or for a single person to find a spouse. For any or all of these things the pastor may yearn, and will consequently turn that yearning into prayer. Yearning is part of pastoring, and no pastor who truly loves her flock will be immune from it.

The hurting heart of a pastor

Yearning can take a deeper turn, in which the pastor finds himself facing not just longing for others but pain. Paul was no stranger to this experience, either. There are few, if any, pastors who have not experienced pain as a result of their ministry, and it can come from a host of causes. Part of it comes from entering into the pain of others, but another part comes from being the focus of impossible expectations or at the centre of painful misunderstandings and fractured relationships.

You cannot be a pastor without entering into the pain of others. John Pritchard writes:

> Pain-bearing doesn't sound like a very welcome part of a priestly task, but it is a huge service to people and communities. The pain comes in many forms in a broken world with wounded people. Priests are not made of iron; they share brokenness with everyone else. But their special dark privilege is to be pain bearers, keeping vigil with a damaged world until God finally puts all the world to rights.[37]

At the extreme, we may have seen pastors or priests caught in the centre of tragedy and so focusing the sorrow of their communities, expressing the deeply held hurt and faith of stricken people—such as in Dunblane after the shootings in 1996, or in Soham after the murder of two schoolchildren in 2002. In both cases, the clergy became a sort of lightning rod for the grief and trauma as the community came to terms with such evil happening in their quiet towns.

On a lesser scale (though no less painful for the individuals concerned), most pastors will enter into the pain of untimely bereavement, the death of a child or a stillbirth, suicide, the sudden onset of chronic or fatal illness or some other accident or tragedy. In these circumstances, the pastor will become a pain bearer, feeling with the sufferer, communicating that emotion to others in the church fellowship, and often being deeply affected himself. The pastor will not be able to offer any answers, but he may be able to mobilise help; his tears will mingle with those of the sufferers, even though he realises that he does not bear the acute grief himself. He will be no stranger to pain and loss.

A pastor can also be a pain bearer in another, less obvious way—that is, if she is the focus of misunderstanding, unrealistic or wrong expectations, or conflict. This may result from what she herself has done or from what she has failed to do. I well remember the pain of receiving a letter from a member of a former church, who criticised my failure to acknowledge through pastoral ministry the loss of one of their parents. They pointed out my failure and added that, as a result, they would be leaving the church. There may, of course, have been wider issues involved—I shall never really know—but it was a painful situation to handle as a young pastor, wondering how I could have failed to spot their need or whether I was the target of unrealistic expectations or a hidden agenda.

Like many other pastors, I have experienced painful episodes in which misunderstandings have crept in, often early in ministry in a new place, leading to resignations from church councils and sometimes descriptions of the pastor that are less than flattering and, frankly, hard to understand. This is because, in part, as a church leader you are a lightning rod for wider feelings about the church as a whole, which go beyond your own style or conduct. Rather than taking these emotions personally, you must recognise that you are simply earthing disappointment or even anger. With experience, this will become easier, and your understandable feelings of injustice can in turn be earthed by sharing them with a spiritual director. Such an experience is not so very far removed from Jesus', yet 'when they hurled their insults at him, he did not retaliate; when he suffered, he made no threats. Instead, he entrusted himself to him who judges justly' (1 Peter 2:23).

Paul surely would have agreed with this model, too.

Paul himself was no stranger to pain in ministry, resulting from misunderstanding or wrong expectations. As we have seen in Chapter 8, this was especially true in connection with the Corinthian church. Somehow, his relationship with the Corinthians was always tense and prone to misunderstanding. The pain caused by this group was the most personal; they questioned his style, his apostleship, his effectiveness and his genuineness—and he pointed out their failings, their love of flamboyance and their superficiality. With other churches that caused him grief, the differences appear less personal and more to do with the believers deserting or distorting the gospel (for example, the Galatian and Colossian churches respectively), so Paul's distress, though great, was not so personally focused. He was astonished and alarmed but not personally attacked.

You could be forgiven for thinking that the work of a pastor is something to be avoided rather than embraced, what with the yearning and the pain, but that is less than half the story. The other part is that to be a pastor is to enter into a unique relationship of trust with people, where you become party to their most profound struggles, and this is an extraordinary privilege. It may entail understanding something of their past and the wounds that it may have inflicted, journeying with them to wholeness, helping with the process of giving or offering forgiveness so that they may experience freedom, peace and release, or encouraging them to take a step, however difficult, which is simply the right thing to do. Although there may be difficulties on the way in any of these circumstances, the pastor, like Paul himself, will experience three sustaining and rewarding emotions, which we will now consider—affection, thankfulness and hope.

The affectionate heart of a pastor

Paul wore his heart on his sleeve. Far from being a cold-hearted misogynist, as he is sometimes wrongly depicted, he was a very warm-hearted man with deep understanding and passionate aspirations for the church and everyone in it to be all that they could and should be. The signs of this affection are not hard to find, although, in his correspondence with the Corinthians and Galatians especially, it can be masked by the issues of truth or church practice with which he had to deal. Even in these more troubled relationships, however, Paul particularly extols the power and importance of love. After all, as we have already seen, it is while writing to the Corinthians about the use of spiritual gifts that he describes the 'most excellent way' of love (1 Corinthians 13), considered by many to be the most important description of love in the Bible. Equally, in bringing back the Galatians to a true faith, he gives us the foundational principle that 'the only thing that counts is faith expressing itself through love' (Galatians 5:6b). In three of Paul's epistles—to the Philippians, Thessalonians and Ephesians—his affection is very much part of his relationship with them and he is pleased to show it.

The Philippian and Thessalonian churches seem to have had a special place in Paul's affections. Visits to both these communities came at the beginning of his second missionary journey and took place despite fierce opposition. In Philippi, Paul ended up in gaol, and in Thessalonica, his next port of call, he was opposed by vociferous Jews who stirred up the whole town against him so that he had to leave after three sabbaths. Despite this opposition, or maybe because of it, churches were founded in both these Roman colonies in Greece, to which Paul was deeply attached.

In writing to the Philippians he says, 'It is right for me to feel this way about all of you, since I have you in my heart... God can testify how I long for all of you with the affection of Christ Jesus' (1:7–8) The Greek word for 'affection' here literally means 'bowels': it describes a feeling coming from the pit of his stomach, the depth of his being. The same idea occurs in the Gospels, when Jesus feels compassion for an individual (see John 11:33): once again it is felt in the bowels, the depth of his being. Out of this strong affection Paul prayed for the Philippians, 'that your love may abound more and more in knowledge and depth of insight' (1:9). This prayer was born out of a profound affection, like that of Christ Jesus, which led to a desire that their own love would deepen and mature.

Paul also had great affection for the Thessalonians. Recalling how that feeling was expressed from his very earliest contact with them, he writes, 'We were gentle among you, like a mother caring for her little children. We loved you so much that we were delighted to share with you not only the gospel of God but our lives as well, because you had become so dear to us' (1 Thessalonians 2:7–8). Here is no cold-hearted disciplinarian but a tender, passionate, warm and affectionate pastor and friend. He goes on to say, 'We dealt with each of you as a father deals with his own children, encouraging, comforting and urging you to live lives worthy of God, who calls you into his kingdom and glory' (vv. 11–12). Paul's model of affectionate pastoring combined the best principles of care present in maternal and paternal nurture, and there is a sense in which pastors of either sex should endeavour to combine in their own nurture both fatherly and motherly care. This is the kind of affection that irradiated Paul's own pastoral care.

An affectionate pastor, then, will seek to care for his flock in many ways, remembering important events, birthdays or significant anniversaries where possible, keeping in touch, giving encouragement and expressing love and affection. I myself have received extraordinary care from my 'line managers'—two Archdeacons in succession, no less, one of whom both sent a card with a warm note in it and telephoned me on my birthday. (Doing this for nearly 100 clergy in his area was a great feat of care and administration.) His successor showed similar care in a different but no less effective way.

We can only suppose that Paul's ability to be affectionate towards his people even during periods of great personal testing, as when he was in gaol in Rome, came from a profound appreciation of God's love. He writes to the Ephesians about comprehending this love: 'I pray that you, being rooted and established in love, may have power, together with all the saints, to grasp how wide and long and high and deep is the love of Christ, and to know this love that surpasses knowledge—that you may be filled to the measure of all the fullness of God' (Ephesians 3:17–19). Sadly, the Ephesians must have failed over time to grasp the full extent of this love, for they were charged in Revelation 2:4 with losing their own first love. But Paul himself had such a revelation of the love of God, in both its purity and its mercy, that it fired his affection for the churches and suffused his messages to them. It produced in him an affection that drove him to prayer for them and made him yearn for contact with them (1 Thessalonians 2:17–18). Such genuine affection cannot be manufactured but, where it exists, it is a most powerful bond in pastoral care, which ties the cared-for and the pastor in bonds of mutual love.

The thankful heart of a pastor

Arriving at the morning worship service one day, I met an older member of our congregation who had not been there for a few weeks. She said how good it was to be back, how much she had missed being able to attend and how wonderful the community was. Music to any pastor's ears—but by the evening I was more than conscious of other members of the church who had serious difficulties with still other members of it. As pastors, we are dealing with the human family, after all—Christians, yes, but still needing help to apply principles of Christian lifestyle to everyday situations that can get very painful.

Even so, looking out at a congregation and knowing something of the struggles and heartaches of many, who are still there to worship and listen to the voice of God, is to be filled with gratitude for the privilege of shepherding God's flock. When the eminent 18th-century evangelical leader Henry Venn was ordained, Charles Simeon, the equally well-known vicar of Holy Trinity Cambridge (famed for his preaching and pastoral ministry), wrote, 'I congratulate you not on a permission to receive £40 or £50 a year, nor on the title of reverend, but on your accession to the most valuable, most honourable, most important, most glorious office in the world to that of ambassador of the Lord Jesus Christ.'[38] The privilege remains, whatever the difficulties, and that privilege is to apply the grace of God as a medicine to the fears, failures and joys of human life. More than that, it is to see grace bring transformation to the lives of others—hope instead of fear; peace instead of guilt; purpose instead of futility; reconciliation instead of alienation.

Paul saw repeatedly the way in which the gospel transformed lives. Once again, he recalled how, during his short stay with the Thessalonians, 'you turned to God from idols to serve the living and true God' (1 Thessalonians 1:9b). He went on to say, 'For what is our hope, our joy, or crown in which we will glory in the presence of our Lord Jesus when he comes? Is it not you? Indeed, you are our glory and joy' (2:19–20). The fruits of the labour of this evangelist-pastor were the people themselves—these 'living letters', as he calls the Corinthian Christians (see 2 Corinthians 3:3), who commended both the gospel and Paul's ministry—and therefore he was eternally grateful to God for the privilege of ministry.

The hopeful heart of a pastor

I don't think you can be a pastor unless you have hope in your heart. And what kind of hope would that be? The hope that every and any situation is susceptible to prayer; the hope that God is able to bring reconciliation and redemption to human relationships; the hope that God's grace can break down barriers. To be a pastor without this kind of hope would be like setting sail without a breath of wind or beginning a walk under dark clouds and the promise of heavy rain. It is the hope of change, the hope that God himself will intervene, that sustains the pastor in his or her ministry.

Paul himself was full of hope, and this is shown especially in the epistle to the Romans. He talks there of every Christian's hope giving him or her the prospect of glory and also being the product of perseverance in the context of suffering (5:2b–5). This hope will not prove a disappointment, because God's love has been poured out by the Spirit into our hearts. In chapter 8 of the same epistle, hope plays a key role in enabling the Christian to live in the 'now' of suffering, difficulty and mortality while awaiting the 'not yet' of what has been promised: 'For in this hope we were saved. But hope that is seen is no hope at all. Who hopes for what he already has? But if we hope for what we do not yet have, we wait for it patiently' (vv. 24–25).

This hope, which is a confident expectation of what is promised us in Christ despite the contrary signals of the present time, must be part of every Christian's armoury. For pastors, it must be especially so, for they must frequently minister hope in times of acute difficulty. Their message will be one of holding on to this hope despite occasionally having to face intense disappointment or tragedy. I was recently on a SOMA[39] ministry trip in Uganda at the invitation of the acting Bishop of Rwenzori Diocese. The previous bishop, Patrick, had been a remarkable leader but he had been killed in a road traffic accident just one year into his episcopate and a few months before we visited, leaving a wife and three children. One of the team I took on the trip had tragically lost his only daughter in her gap year, also in a road accident. Out of a sense of his own pain and loss, he was able to minister to and pastor the Ugandan diocese in their loss, reminding them of the hope we have in Christ while fully acknowledging their present sufferings. It was a case of a pastor with both pain and hope in his heart, ministering hope to those still caught up in the pain and bewilderment of loss.

In a very sensitive way—initially not even with words but simply with presence and love—a pastor can be a symbol of hope as well as a pain-bearer, as we have already noted. Paul all but concludes his great epistle to the Romans with this prayer: 'May the God of hope fill you with all joy and peace as you trust in him, so that you may overflow with hope by the power of the Holy Spirit' (15:13). Overflowing with hope is not a bad description of an effective pastor's heart—otherwise he might be crushed by the load.

Chapter 11

The pastor as mentor

There is no occupation quite like pastoral ministry for sharing deeply with others, knowing the good and the bad, the fears and the hopes, the challenges and the possibilities. So, in turn, the pastor's heart must be refreshed and strengthened, whether by good spiritual direction, family life, activities that take her away from the intensity of some of this ministry, enjoyment of creation and times of quiet prayer and reflection. Without these, the task could be overwhelming, but, with some or any of them, the grace of God can lighten the burden, point the way and refresh the heart. At the end of it all, we must realise that we are not indispensable but are part of a chain of pastoral care extending over the generations, given to care for particular people in our time. To this end we train others also, becoming a mentor to a few who will carry on the vision of teaching and care to which we have been committed, while no doubt expanding, adapting and applying it in new ways to succeeding generations. Ministering to the many but focusing on the few is part of the spiritual economy of being a pastor.

Paul knew that he must pass his message and ministry on to others. After all, while lengthy and profound in its impact, his ministry could not have lasted more than 35 years in total, including the time of preparation. He knew that time would be short, circumstances were difficult, churches must be led and new areas reached. He therefore needed to train others (see 2 Timothy 2:2, 14). The tradition of training disciples was, in fact, well founded in Israel, being common among the rabbinic schools. As we have seen, Paul himself had been trained in Jerusalem as a young man among the followers of Rabbi Hillel, under the leadership of Gamaliel. Rabbis would have a group of followers who devoted themselves to their master's teaching, and so Jesus' model of appointing and training twelve disciples was not unusual. It was in this tradition that Paul set about training others for the task of Christian ministry.

Generally speaking, it appears that Paul had two circles of colleagues and associates. The wider circle were people whom he knew and loved as fellow followers of the Way but who were not necessarily close colleagues or associates being trained by him for future ministry. Many in this category are found in the long list at the end of Romans 16. Thought to have been written between AD57 and 59, quite possibly in Corinth (see the mention of Erastus, the city treasurer of Corinth, in Romans 16:23), the epistle to the Romans shows the extent of the fellowship that existed some seven or eight years after the start of Paul's second missionary journey and his ministry in Europe. Most of those on the list are not people mentioned by Luke as accompanying Paul on his missionary journeys. Only the redoubtable Priscilla and Aquila, wholehearted and wise in their service, who had risked their lives for Paul (16:3–4), are mentioned in Acts, because they had corrected Apollos' misunderstanding in the faith (Acts 18:24–26). Nevertheless, the list in Romans 16 witnesses to the growing Christian community throughout the empire, both its fluidity and its close bonds. Alongside this group, who were no doubt deeply influenced by the example of Paul's life, was a smaller group of associates— people whom he was actively preparing for leadership in the church and upon whom he personally depended.

From Luke's account of the missionary journeys in Acts, it seems that these associates were about six in number: John Mark, Timothy, Silas, Titus, Ephaphras and Epaphroditus, each of whom had a slightly different role and ministry. Their characters and backgrounds were also distinctly different and Paul's influence on them varied in its extent as well as its success.

John Mark

The case of John Mark was both problematic and promising. John Mark was a cousin of Barnabas (Colossians 4:10). He is traditionally considered to be the author of the second Gospel, turning the memoirs of the apostle Peter into a racy and dynamic account. As a very young man he was present at the arrest of Jesus in Gethsemane but escaped by slipping out of his robe when seized by the temple guard, and so fled naked (Mark 14:51–52). He accompanied Paul and Barnabas on the first missionary journey but later deserted Paul at Perga (Acts 13:13) and returned to Jerusalem. When it came to the second missionary journey, Barnabas wanted to take John Mark along, but Paul refused. As a result, the two of them had a fierce argument and separated (15:39). Paul was not prepared to expose his missionary journey to any future desertion or disloyalty by Mark, but Barnabas was more than prepared to give his cousin a second chance. It was a clash of principles, neither of which was wrong—demonstrating that dissension is easy for two people who hold passionately to differing but laudable views that are integral to their own motivation, when neither of them can back down.

Happily, the story does not end there. We find Mark working again with Paul as one of his associates towards the end of his ministry in Rome, from where Paul hopes to send Mark to Colossae (Colossians 4:10). He is mentioned with other close colleagues of Paul in Philemon 24 and, finally, Paul tells Timothy, presumably in Ephesus, to send Mark to him since 'he is helpful to me in my ministry' (2 Timothy 4:11). Whatever the break in their relationship, it had by then been patched up. Both their hearts were set on serving their Lord—which was not the case, for instance, with Demas, also mentioned in Philemon 24, who, by Paul's second letter to Timothy had 'deserted' Paul as he 'loved this world' (4:10).

The relationship of John Mark to Paul perhaps indicates that Paul was demanding but also quickly forgiving in his relationship with a younger mentee who had not lived up to his exacting expectations. John Mark had been entirely taken into Paul's confidence and apostolic work during Paul's first missionary journey, so his training came from a complete involvement with Paul in action as a pioneer evangelist, church planter and pastor. His training was 'on the job', involving close personal contact, continuous observation of Paul's methods and ample opportunity to reflect and discuss with Paul as they travelled by boat or by foot.

Timothy

Although Paul evidently placed the work of the gospel above personal considerations, his relationship with Timothy shows the lengths to which he would go in training and shaping a future church leader. Of the six close associates whom we have identified as receiving both direction and training by Paul, the closest to him was Timothy. In some ways it seems an unequal relationship—the hugely able, intellectual, physically courageous and formidable personality of Paul contrasting with the weak, timid, more dependent personality of Timothy. Yet, however different they were, Paul recognised in Timothy a potential leader of the church.

Timothy came from the town of Lystra near Iconium, in present-day southern Turkey but then in the province of Galatia. Despite his strictures about the Galatian churches' reversion to Judaism and insistence on circumcision, Paul, amazingly, circumcised Timothy to make him more acceptable to the Jews from a missional perspective, since it was known that his father was a Greek (Acts 16:3; see 1 Corinthians 9:20). (It would not, of course, make him in any way more acceptable to God: Galatians 6:15.) Soon Timothy became a close colleague, revisiting with Paul several of the towns visited on the first missionary journey (Acts 16:3–4) before going with him to Greece on the second missionary journey. We find him at Thessalonica, Berea, Athens and Corinth (Acts 17:14–15; 18:5), and presumably he was at Philippi, though not arrested like Paul and Silas. On the third of Paul's missionary journeys, Timothy went to Ephesus—where quite possibly he was detained with Paul (see 2 Corinthians 1:8–10)—and then returned to Macedonia (Acts 19:22). He was also sent as an emissary to Corinth (1 Corinthians 16:10–11), carrying Paul's first letter to them.

In Paul, Timothy found the strong mentor he may have been subconsciously looking for, who would strengthen his naturally trusting and sensitive nature, bending it to the demanding task of pastoring a church in first-century Ephesus in a by-and-large hostile environment.

Paul's mentoring was not of the indirect kind; his spiritual direction was very much 'direction'! Eugene Peterson says that spiritual direction takes place 'when two people agree to give their full attention to what God is doing in one or both of their lives and seek to respond in faith'.[40] Paul certainly gave his undivided attention to the task that faced Timothy and also to the resources he would need to discharge it. If we look over Paul's letters to Timothy, we can see that beside the specific instruction given for the conduct of the church, Paul gives personal advice to Timothy along the lines of his gifting, his character and the holiness of his life.

Timothy's gifts appear to be of the classic pastor/teacher kind. He probably did not excel, as far as we can see, either as a church-planting evangelist or as a prophet but rather as a teacher and conserver of the faith passed down to him. Repeatedly—especially in his second letter to Timothy, which is more personal than the first—Paul tells him 'to guard the good deposit' (orthodox teaching and practice) as well as passing it on to others who would faithfully teach yet others (2 Timothy 1:14; 2:2). His gifts as a teacher were to be actively and courageously deployed, in a single-minded fashion (2:4–7).

Much of Paul's mentoring was therefore about strengthening Timothy's resolve. It is here that we see mentoring at its most personal, Paul recognising Timothy's temptation to be timid, inviting him to rely on the Spirit (2 Timothy 1:7) and showing how he must be prepared, if necessary, to suffer and endure his share of difficulties. Paul's exhortation is generously peppered with lessons from his own experience (see 2:9–10; 3:10–11; 4:6–8, 16–18) to give Timothy an inspiring example to follow.

Lastly Paul attends to Timothy's personal holiness or dedication to the task. He is to be 'kind to everyone' (2 Timothy 2:24); he is to avoid disputes about words (1 Timothy 6:3–5; 2 Timothy 2:14), shun any immoderate behaviour of youth (2:22) and look to himself, taking care of his bodily needs (1 Timothy 5:23). Paul's mentoring therefore involved all-round counsel, being both well targeted and affectionate. It sprang from constant prayer and from bonds of affection, evidenced by Timothy's tears (2 Timothy 1:4), quite possibly when Paul left him and the others at Miletus (Acts 20:4, 37) before returning to Jerusalem.

Paul's other companions

Although Paul had a number of other companions, such as Epaphroditus from Philippi, Sopater from Berea and Epaphras from the Lycus valley (who were instrumental in beginning churches in Colossae, Hierapolis and Laodicea respectively), there were two other close associates on whom he particularly relied: Titus and Silas.

Titus does not appear in Acts but went with Paul and Barnabas to Jerusalem to present the Gentile issue to the apostles (Galatians 2:1). He was a Greek convert to Judaism and appears to have been a capable administrator, a safe pair of hands, entrusted with Paul's second (but lost) severe letter to the Corinthians (see 2 Corinthians 2:3). When Titus returned to Paul in Macedonia (see 7:6), Paul then wrote his more emollient letter to the church at Corinth, known to us as 2 Corinthians. He did this after conferring with Titus and gaining insight into the state of the Corinthian church.

Titus was, for a time, the pastor of the church in Crete, to which he and Paul may have gone at some point and where he was charged to set up leadership in the church and straighten up their doctrine and lifestyle. Finally, we hear of him evangelising in Dalmatia (2 Timothy 4:10b).

Besides Titus there was Silas, a fellow Roman citizen from the Jerusalem church. After the split with Barnabas and Mark, Silas accompanied Paul on his second missionary journey, being imprisoned with him at Philippi and then going to

Thessalonica, Berea, Athens and Corinth. He was to remain an important link between Paul and the Corinthian church. Like John Mark, he eventually gravitated to Rome, where we hear of him helping Peter with his letters (see 1 Peter 5:13).

Among all these colleagues, as well as the wider circle of friends, Paul was the yardstick by which they measured both the orthodoxy of their teaching and the pattern of their lives. His example would remain the compelling standard of life and ministry for ages to come. He also stands as an example to pastors today, in that we too should prepare others for leadership through mentoring. If the apostle had only five or six whom he closely mentored, among a much wider group whom he no doubt inspired, we as pastors today should focus on a few who will be leaders in the church of the future and invest in them. If this was done uniformly by leaders, what a resource would be prepared for the future ministry of the church!

Conclusion

As mentioned at the outset of this book, we may not think of Paul primarily as a pastor. He was a church planter or evangelist par excellence: his style of evangelism was not so much about adding individuals to the churches by challenging them to come to faith (although there are several examples of that); rather, he gathered new communities to God through the preaching of Jesus as the Christ and through powerful encounters with the kingdom of God (see Romans 15:17–20). Paul was also an extraordinary teacher, unsurpassed in the two millennia of Christian history since then, explaining the gospel to the various mindsets present in his world, whether Jew or Gentile. In addition, he had prophetic insight into the 'end times', without any crude timetable attached. All this was incorporated into his apostolic ministry, exercised with an authority and vocation given to him by Christ in that encounter on the Damascus road. And included in the fivefold ministry advocated by Paul himself (see Ephesians 4:11), which is necessary for leadership of the church in every age, was his pastoral care, which was second to none.

When we consider Paul as a pastor, he shows us that the object of pastoral care is to enable freedom and maturity both in the individual Christian and in the community of the church. Freedom comes in many shapes and sizes, often defined by freedom *from* something as well as freedom *for* something. We see Paul teaching that freedom for the Jew is freedom from the law, in the sense that we cease to justify ourselves by it; for others it is freedom from false asceticism or religion, while for still others it is freedom from control by selfish habits or from fear, anxiety or slavishly following human demands. In the end, freedom means simply being ourselves, as God has made us and wants us to be—fulfilling that risky saying of Augustine, 'Love God and do what you like.'

Alongside freedom, we see the other chief objective of Paul's pastoral care, which is maturity—expressed several times, not least to the Colossians and Ephesians (Colossians 1:28; 2:2; Ephesians 4:11–16). This maturity is one of faith or understanding as well as character, so Paul is always most concerned with what we think about God, the gospel, ourselves, our calling and the church, and these themes occur again and again. Our thinking is the most powerful activity of our personality, so guiding, forming and correcting our thinking is an essential part of growth to maturity. Paul never left the churches he pastored unchallenged in their thinking, especially if he perceived that it was deficient in some way.

Maturity is also a matter of developing character, particularly in bearing with difficulties and struggles in life. The Christian character is constantly the object of Paul's attention in his epistles. We see repeated use of such words as gratitude, love, gentleness, faithfulness and endurance, all of which were attitudes that he sought to foster in individuals and churches. Maturity in both understanding and character remain the object of the pastor today, so he or she must not only empathise and sympathise but also challenge and, where necessary, call for change.

Paul remains an inspiration to all pastors—one to be studied and emulated, fathomed and then followed. Yesterday I had a typical Sunday. It began with a quiet 8 o'clock Holy

Communion for ten people, including a couple worshipping with us for the first time, having recently arrived from South Africa. After breakfast I went to preach in a neighbouring parish that is currently without a vicar; in so doing, I met a congregation of older people as well as many young families seeking admission to the very good local church school. I had lunch at home with a couple facing some pressures and a young man with some health problems. A call from our local hospital summoned me to the bedside of a dying woman whose family became estranged from the church when it changed its style of worship 25 years ago. I prayed for her and encouraged the family to return to church, telling them that there was space for all sorts and styles of worship now. Then I looked in at the Acute Stroke Unit to see the radiant smile of one older and much-loved member of the church who had suffered a stroke ten days before. She could not move much but could utter one word—'Yes'—and her eyes and smile spoke of hope and assurance. After that, I went to our evening service, mostly full of younger people, congratulating two young women on their recent engagements and admiring their rings. My day finished at 10pm after talking with a couple about an issue they faced concerning forgiveness.

Almost all of life in a day! Who else would minister healing, reconciliation and hope to the dying, teach about giving, share the joy of two engagements, hear about the pain of broken relationships and welcome new people from across the world?

Fundamentally, the model for pastoral care—indeed, the language for pastoral care—derived from Paul is love. And its basis is faith, because without the intervention of God, nothing lasting can be achieved. Since pastoring is about enabling transformation into Christ's likeness, which is our final goal, we will finish with Paul's words—and to whom else but those troublesome Corinthians, the grit in the oyster shell of his ministry, who thus created pearls of teaching and character. He wrote, 'We, who with unveiled faces all reflect the Lord's glory, are being transformed into his likeness with ever-increasing glory, which comes from the Lord, who is the Spirit' (2 Corinthians 3:18). In the final analysis, the pastor is the privileged servant of that process, a co-worker with the Spirit, enabling one more degree of change along the path to true freedom and lasting maturity. To share in that process, however exacting, is a noble calling and a privilege indeed.

Study guide

Chapter 1: The making of a pastor (Acts 9:1–31)

- As we have seen in this chapter, Paul was shaped for his ministry a long time before he became a follower of the Way. How was God at work in him, preparing him for his future role and ministry?

- Can you discern ways in which, through heredity, family background, education and gifting, you have been prepared for the ministry you now have?

- Most conversions tend to be gradual and definitely not as dramatic as Paul's. Do you know of occasions when people have turned to God more suddenly and dramatically? Are there reasons for this? Should we be more expectant of sudden conversion than we are?

- Paul spent three years in the wilderness of Arabia after his initial reception and his preaching in Damascus. This wilderness or desert experience seems akin in type to Jesus' own time in the wilderness, when he was tempted. What purpose did this period of withdrawal serve in Paul's life? Are there similar experiences that have been important in your own preparation for ministry?

- Summarise the ways in which God was preparing Paul for his ministry and what we might learn from that in our own preparation for ministry. Are there lessons to be drawn?

Chapter 2: A ministry of all the talents (Ephesians 4:1-16)

- The fivefold ministry of apostle, prophet, evangelist, pastor and teacher appears to be the essential and necessary leadership team for the local church. Which of these ministries seem to be neglected today, and why might that be? What does your own local church lack, and how could that ministry be encouraged?

- The three most unusual ministries of the five are probably apostle, prophet and evangelist. If they were more common, what effect would they have on the church? How might they be encouraged more?

- What difficulties of understanding do you have with any of these ministries?

- Why do you think pastor and teacher are often linked together?

- Do you think, from your knowledge of Paul, that he was equally strong in all these ministries?

Chapter 3: Right thinking (Galatians 3:1-14; 4:8-20)

- We don't live in an age that is characterised by the challenging of wrong ideas. Why is that?

- Pastoral care is not generally associated with challenging wrong thinking. Why is that?

- What would you say is the goal of pastoral care? Would you say that developing freedom and maturity was the aim of Paul's pastoral care or would you describe it as something else?

- Paul risked a lot in tackling the issues, but he risked much more by not tackling them. What puts off pastors from tackling issues, and is there anything we can learn from Paul about the way he tackled them?

- As well as the issues of 'right thinking' or good practice mentioned in this chapter, are there others that Paul tackled, maybe especially in the Corinthian correspondence, which should be recalled as examples of establishing good pastoral care?

Chapter 4: Right attitudes and lifestyle (Romans 12:1–21)

- Why should a pastor concern herself with right attitudes? What attitudes ruin a church? What attitudes make a church?

- What is the connection between doctrine and attitudes? How is this shown particularly in Philippians 2:1–17? Can you think of any other examples from the epistles, in which doctrine is seen to be the source of right attitudes?

- If thankfulness, humility, perseverance and gentleness are important characteristics of any church community, how best are they grown?

- The trilogy of faith, hope and love is often used by Paul to describe genuine Christian living (see 1 Thessalonians 1:3). What is the relationship between the three of them?

- Do you agree with Paul that the only thing that matters in church life is 'faith expressing itself through love' (Galatians 5:6b)?

Chapter 5: Right relationships

If you are following these studies in a home group that meets weekly, you may want to cover these questions over two or more weeks, as the issues covered are so substantial.

Marriage and singleness
(Ephesians 5:21–33; 1 Corinthians 7:1–7)

- In what ways does the Hebrew view of marriage differ from the Roman view of marriage?

- Do you agree that husband and wife are to submit to each other, and how might that work in practice?

- Do you agree that both the husband's call to love his wife and the wife's call to submit to her husband have the common root of 'selfless self-giving to each other' and are therefore two sides of the same coin?

- How can the church be more supportive of single people?

Homosexuality (Romans 1:24–32)

- Do you think that there is any difference between the practice of homosexuality in the Greco-Roman world and today? If so, what difference does that make?

- If a gay couple asked for a blessing of their civil partnership in your church, what answer would you give and why?

- How would you set about helping a Christian couple whom you know well if one of their children announced themselves gay and said that now the church would only judge them?

Divorce (1 Corinthians 7:8–16)
- On what grounds would Paul have sanctioned divorce?

- Do you think your pastor should remarry divorcees, provided that neither party was instrumental in the break-up of their previous marriages?

- In what ways can support be given to married couples in your church? What exists at the moment? What more might be done? What role might the pastor have in this?

Authority (1 Corinthians 11:3–16)
- In Paul's day, there was a clear structure in the household with regard to authority. This was given visible expression, for women, by wearing head coverings and, for men by taking teaching roles in the church (see 1 Corinthians 11:3–16; 1 Timothy 2:9–10). What relevance, if any, does this teaching have in today's very different society?

- What do you think Paul's attitude was to slavery? Do you think he was too acquiescent or do you think that he had a strategy for its ending? (See Philemon.)

- What was Paul's view of the function of the state (see Romans 13:1–7)? Are there occasions when the state forfeits any right to cooperation? What kind of resistance is permissible?

Chapter 6: Right leadership (2 Corinthians 5:11–21)

- If the pastor is regarded as the church leader, she or he will be involved in many ministries in it—administration, strategic leadership, teaching, reconciliation and so on. Can one person undertake all these ministries? What model of pastoral leadership in the church would you advise?

- What are the ingredients that make for effective reconciliation? Can you give examples from your life of either successful or unsuccessful reconciliation? What have you learnt from these examples?

- Do you believe in the power of presence? What does the presence of the leader/pastor bring to the church community? What spiritual dynamic does their presence bring?

- Have you come across any modern-day issues that relate to the idea of 'the strong' and the 'weak' conscience? Can you say what they are, and how differences have been resolved with regard to them?

- Why do some pastors find it difficult to collaborate? Is there anything that can be done about that?

Chapter 7: Prayer
(Ephesians 6:18–20; 2 Corinthians 12:1–10)

- What do you think might have been the main differences between Paul's prayers as an orthodox Pharisee and as a Christian?

- In what ways did the needs of the churches focus Paul's praying? What can we learn from that? Do we ever stop to ask how we can best pray for a church that we are connected to in any way?

- Would you describe Paul as a mystic? How would you describe the tradition of mystic prayer in the church? What does it especially bring to the life of prayer?

- Often we struggle to deepen the prayer life of churches. What kind of praying is appealing today? What kind of prayer events have inspired you, and why?

- What pattern of personal prayer works for you? If there is one thing you could do to deepen your prayer life, what would it be?

Chapter 8: Strength and weakness
(2 Corinthians 12:7b–10)

- Can you identify particular qualities that are perceived as strengths and weaknesses in today's world?

- What do you think Paul meant by 'weakness'? Consider the main passages that deal with this topic and reflect on them (Philippians 2:1–11; 2 Corinthians 4:7–18; 11:21—12:10). What insights do these passages give us into Paul's concept of weakness?

- Can anyone in the group give any examples of how, although feeling weak, they were actually strong in terms of ministry?

- Why should weakness lead to strength? What role does the grace of God have in this (2 Corinthians 12:1–10). Are we left sometimes with things we must bear rather than having them removed—for example, in relation to health, personal circumstances and so on?

- In what ways did Jesus himself exemplify the teaching of being strong in weakness?

Chapter 9: Word and sacraments
(Colossians 2:6–15; 2 Timothy 3:10—4:8)

- In what contexts does the pastor rely on the word of God—for example in shaping his or her life, in teaching, in forming aspirations for individuals and the community, in personal counselling and in training others?

- In what ways does the pastor rely on the Spirit in terms of understanding, gifting, discernment and transformational change?

- Would you say you were more 'word' than 'Spirit' or more 'Spirit' than 'word'? Why is there sometimes a division between people of the word and people of the Spirit? What can be done to make us both 'word and Spirit' people?

- What were the main points of Paul's teaching on baptism (see, for example, Romans 6) and on the Lord's Supper (see, for example, 1 Corinthians 10:14–17; 11:17–34)?

- What role do sacraments play in your life and your church's life? Do you think that the attention to each in your fellowship is about right?

Chapter 10: The pastor's heart
(2 Corinthians 7:2–16)

- Someone once said that every church should have a notice over its entrance, reading, 'Danger—you could be seriously hurt here!' It sounds a bit drastic, but do you think it is true? If so, why? If not, why not? What has your experience of church been? Why are churches places of joy but also, sometimes, pain?

- Is it only the pastoral heart that yearns for others? What is special about the pastor's yearning?

- The pastor must discern the difference between fair and unfair expectations—sincere requests for help or, alternatively, requests that are generated by a desire to manipulate or a simple need to 'offload' on the pastor. It has been said that many requests for help or pastoral support can be driven by such things as the need for dependency, power, sex or favour. What advice might be given to the pastor in these situations?

- If your heart is hurt as a pastor, what should you do? What reactions are possible: self-justification, self-criticism or bitterness? How do you avoid negative reactions in relation to being hurt or misunderstood?

- How does a pastor keep her heart full of hope, gratitude and faith?

Chapter 11: The pastor as mentor
(2 Timothy 2:1–7)

- What was the main function and purpose of mentoring for Paul?

- What makes a good mentor?

- What aspects of life and church life should be covered for a person being mentored into pastoral or church leadership?

- How does a busy pastor give time to this aspect of ministry in his work?

- How do we spot people to mentor for the future?

Appendix 1

A service of reconciliation and communion

God gave us the ministry of reconciliation.
2 CORINTHIANS 5:18

Scriptures

'Lord, how many times shall I forgive my brother when he sins against me? Up to seven times?' Jesus answered, 'I tell you, not seven times, but seventy-seven times.'
MATTHEW 18:21–22

'First go and be reconciled to your brother or sister; then come and offer your gift.'
MATTHEW 5:24

'Come to me, all you who are weary and burdened, and I will give you rest. Take my yoke upon you and learn from me, for I am gentle and humble in heart, and you will find rest for your souls. For my yoke is easy and my burden is light.'
MATTHEW 11:28–30

Acknowledgment of past hurt

Having written a narrative of all the ways we have experienced hurt or pain from each other, we hand the scripts to the minister.

Taking these scripts, we say together:

All these pains and hurts: we cast on the cross.
All these wounds and failures: we cast on the cross.
All these offences and shortcomings: we cast on the cross.

The minister then burns the narratives of 'hurts and pains' and scatters the ashes around the cross.

Prayer of confession (each party)

Lord Jesus, forgive us all the ways, both knowing and unknowing, that we have hurt M and N: forgive our failures, begin today to renew our trust in one another and draw us close to yourself. Help us now to leave these things behind, as ashes in the past, and move into your future for our lives. In your name. Amen

An absolution prayer by the minister

A moment of silence

We are not enemies: we are fellow disciples of Christ.
We are not adversaries: we are sinners cleansed by grace.
We are not strangers: we have been made members of the body of Christ for ever.

The Peace

We exchange the Peace together.

Communion

Say Eucharistic Prayer G from *Common Worship*.
   We offer the bread and wine to each other

The blessing

Christ crucified draw you to himself, to find in him a sure ground for faith, a firm support for hope and the assurance of sins forgiven; and the blessing of God almighty, the Father, the Son and the Holy Spirit be amongst you and remain with you and all those whom you love now and always. Amen

Appendix 2
Mentoring

The following are questions that might be used during a mentoring session with someone, once a relationship of mentoring has been established. Meetings are probably best held around three or four times a year.

- In what ways do you discern God working in your life at the moment?
- What challenges or issues do you have to face presently?
- Are there any areas in your relationships that need to be taken forward or resolved?
- How do you see things working out in your life over the next six months? What are the priorities that you would give yourself?
- In what ways are you using your gifts in the workplace, community or church presently?
- Are you being called to give up or take up anything at the moment?
- How is your prayer life developing at present? What do you think would refresh and invigorate or sustain you? What resources might you put in place to enable this?
- Is God speaking through his word or Spirit in any particular way at the moment?

Bibliography

F.F. Bruce, *The Apostle of the Free Spirit*, Paternoster Press, 1977.

Lavinia Byrne, *Original Prayer*, SPCK, 2008.

Colin Chapman, *Whose Promised Land?* Lion, 2002.

Donald Coggan, *Paul: Portrait of a Revolutionary*, Hodder and Stoughton, 1984.

James Denny, *The Death of Christ*, Tyndale Press, 1956.

Esther de Waal, *Seeking God*, Canterbury Press, 1999.

James D.G. Dunn, *The Theology of Paul the Apostle*, Eerdmans, 2006.

Gordon Fee, *God's Empowering Presence*, Hendrickson, 1994.

Michael Frost and Alan Hirsch, *The Shaping of Things to Come*, Hendrickson, 2003.

Peter Greig, *God on Mute*, Survivor, 2007.

Tony Horsfall, *Mentoring for Spiritual Growth*, BRF, 2008.

M.R. James, *The Apocryphal New Testament*, OUP, 1924.

Joachim Jeremias, *Jerusalem in the Time of Jesus*, SCM, 1969.

Robin Jewett, *A Chronology of Paul's Life*, Fortress Press, 1979.

Robin Lane Fox, *Pagans and Christians*, Penguin, 1986.

Robin Lane Fox, *The Classical World*, Penguin, 2005.

Elizabeth Ruth Obbard, *Through Julian's Window*, Canterbury Press, 2008.

M. Scott Peck, *The Road Less Travelled*, Arrow, 1978.

St Cyril of Jerusalem (ed. F.L. Cross), *Lectures on the Christian Sacraments*, SPCK, 1980.

E.P. Sanders, *Paul*, OUP, 2001.

Tom Smail, *Praying with Paul*, BRF, 2007.

John Stott, *The Cross of Christ*, IVP, 1986.
John Stott, *The Message of Ephesians*, IVP, 1979.
Stephen Travis, *I Believe in the Second Coming*, Hodder and Stoughton, 1982.
Patrick Whitworth, *Becoming Fully Human*, Terra Nova, 2003.
David Wenham, *Paul and Jesus*, SPCK, 2002.
Tom Wright, *Justification: God's Plan and Paul's Vision*, SPCK, 2009.
N.T. Wright, *Paul: Fresh Perspectives*, SPCK, 2005.
Tom Wright, *Surprised by Hope*, SPCK, 2007.
N.T. Wright, *The Climax of the Covenant*, T&T Clark, 1991.
N.T. Wright, *The New Testament and the People of God*, SPCK, 2002.
Tom Wright, *What St Paul Really Said*, Lion, 1997.
William Paul Young, *The Shack*, Hodder and Stoughton, 2007.

Notes

1. See 'The Acts of Paul and Thecla' in M.R. James, *The Apocryphal New Testament* (OUP, 1924).
2. F.F. Bruce, *The Apostle of the Free Spirit* (Paternoster, 1977), p. 33.
3. Joachim Jeremias, *Jerusalem in the Time of Jesus* (SCM, 1969), p. 242.
4. N.T. Wright, *The New Testament and the People of God* (SPCK, 2002), p. 189.
5. Wright, *New Testament and People of God*, p. 194.
6. Jeremias, *Jerusalem in the Time of Jesus*, pp. 242–243.
7. Wright, *New Testament and People of God*, pp. 187–188.
8. Robin Lane Fox, *The Classical World* (Penguin, 2005), p. 349.
9. Michael Frost and Alan Hirsch, *The Shaping of Things to Come* (Hendrickson, 2003), p. 169.
10. Walter Brueggemann, *Beyond Homelessness* (Eerdmans, 2008).
11. Walter Brueggemann, *Prophetic Imagination* (Fortress Press, 2001), p. 3.
12. See James Fowler, *Stages of Faith: the Psychology of Human Development and the Quest for Meaning* (HarperSanFrancisco, 1995).
13. M. Scott Peck, *The Road Less Travelled* (Arrow, 1978).
14. Alan Jamieson, *A Churchless Faith* (SPCK, 2002), p. 116.
15. James Fowler, *Faith Development and Pastoral Care* (Fortress Press, 1987), p. 93.
16. From Mark's booklet *On My Way to Heaven*.
17. Augustine, Sermon 61.4.
18. Patrick Whitworth, *Prepare for Exile* (SPCK, 2008).
19. For a full treatment of this subject, see Tom Wright, *Surprised by Hope* (SPCK, 2007).
20. Revelations of Divine Love 86:3–4; see Elizabeth Ruth Obbard, *Through Julian's Window* (Canterbury Press, 2008), p. xvi.
21. Lane Fox, *Classical World*, p. 446.
22. J.R.W. Stott, *The Message of Ephesians*, BST (IVP, 1979), p. 235.
23. James D.G. Dunn, *The Theology of Paul the Apostle* (Eerdmans, 2006), p. 690.

24 See Matthew Parris, 'Who's totally gay? There's no straight answer', *The Times* (21 April 2012).
25 Dunn, *Theology of Paul*, p. 699.
26 Lane Fox, *Classical World*, p. 143.
27 William Barclay, *The Letters to the Galatians and Ephesians* (St Andrew Press, 1958), p. 250.
28 Lane Fox, *Classical World*, p. 349.
29 Dunn, *Theology of Paul*, p. 700.
30 Tom Smail, *Praying with Paul* (BRF, 2007), p. 52.
31 Benedicta Ward (trans.), *The Desert Fathers* (Penguin Classics, 2003), p. 65.
32 Dick Eastman, *The Hour that Changes the World* (Baker, 1986).
33 Mike Wenham, *My Donkey Body* (Monarch, 2008).
34 F.L. Cross (ed.), *St Cyril of Jerusalem's Lectures on the Christian Sacraments* (SPCK, 1980), p. xxv.
35 Michael Harper, *Power for the Body of Christ* (Kingsway, 1981), p. 38.
36 Dunn, *Theology of Paul*, p. 396.
37 John Pritchard, *The Life and Work of a Priest*, (SPCK, 2007), p. 66.
38 See John Stott, *I Believe in Preaching* (Hodder & Stoughton, 1982), p. 34).
39 SOMA: Sharing of Ministry Abroad, a cross-cultural Anglican mission agency.
40 Eugene Peterson, *Working the Angles* (Eerdmans, 1987), p. 103; quoted by Tony Horsfall, *Mentoring for Spiritual Growth* (BRF, 2008), p. 14.